Scale of Miles

0   20   40   60   80

MAP NO. EU-7

CLEARTYPE® MAP
PREPARED IN COOPERATION WITH
J. WALTER THOMPSON COMPANY
Ⓒ AMERICAN MAP⁰ CO., INC., N.Y.

B U L G A R I A

DRÁMA   RODHÓPI
RRAI Sidhirókàstron   Drama   Xánthi   Komotiní
Sérrai   Arriana
        Nigríta Kaválla   KAVÁLLA   Sápai   Férrai
Langadhàs Eleytheroúpolis Thásos
Tonika   Stavrós   THÁSOS
saloníki)
KHALKIDHIKÍ   Polýiros   Gulf of Strimón
      MOUNT ATHOS
           Kariaí
      Sykéa

ÉVROS
Orestiás
Dhidhimótikhon
Souflíon

T H R A C E

Alexandroúpolis

Samothrace   Saros Gulf   Dardanelles
SAMOTHRACE

IMBROS

Kástron Moúdhros
        LEMNOS

EVSTRÁTIOS
Vólos
ILIODHROMIA

NORTHERN   SKÍROS

SPORADES

EUBOEA Kími
Istiaía
Aidhipsós

Chalcis
(Khalkís)

Thebes
BOEOTIA & ATTICA
Akharnaí
Elevsís
Mégara   Athens
SALAMIS   (Athínai)
Salamis   Piraeus
AEGINA Koropí Kerátea
Aegina Lávrion
Póros
lion   Saronic
HYDRA   Gulf

Gulf of Édremit
Mithimna
Andissa
LESBOS   LESBOS
Polikhnítos   Mitilíni
Plomárion

Gulf of İzmír

PSARÁ CHIOS
Chíos
CHIOS

T U R K E Y

ÁNDROS
KÉA
TÍNOS
Síros
MÍKONOS

SÁMOS Vathí
SAMOS

IKARÍA

KÍTHNOS SÍROS
C Y C L A D E S
SÉRIFOS PÁROS Náxos
SÍFNOS   NÁXOS
CYCLADES
Mílos ÍOS
MILOS   AMORGÓS

PÁTMOS
LÉROS Léros
Kálimnos
KÁLIMNOS
Kos
KOS

ANÁFI
THIRA

ASTIPALAIA

NÍSIROS   Simi
TELOS   SIMI   Rhodes
DODECANESE   RHODES
KHALKI   Monólito
Cáttavia

SEA OF CANDIA

CR
Canea
(Khaniá)
Kastélli   CANEA
Kandanos   Réthimnon
Khóra   RÉTHIMNI

D1413778

N E A N   N   S E A

The Web of Modern Greek Politics

The Greeks . . . no matter how forlorn their circumstances or how grave the peril to their country, are always divided into many parties, with many leaders who fight among themselves with desperate vigour. . . . The passage of several thousand years sees no change in their characteristics and no diminution of their trials or their vitality. They have survived in spite of all that the world could do against them, and all they could do against themselves. . . . Centuries of foreign rule and indescribable endless oppression leave them still living, active communities and forces in the modern world, quarrelling among themselves with insatiable vivacity. Personally I have always . . . believed in their invincible power to survive internal strife and the world tides threatening their extinction.

Winston S. Churchill, "The Greek Torment,"
Chapter 13 of *Closing the Ring*

The Web of Modern Greek Politics

JANE PERRY CLARK CAREY

&

ANDREW GALBRAITH CAREY

Columbia University Press
New York & London
1968

For the quotation appearing on page ii of this book and taken from Winston Churchill's *Closing the Ring* (1951), Chapter 13, "The Greek Torment," pages 532–533, we are indebted to the publisher, Houghton Mifflin Company of Boston.

To Robert Morrison MacIver

PHILOSOPHER, STUDENT OF LIFE
IN ITS VARIED ASPECTS, TEACHER,
WARM AND INSPIRING PERSONAL FRIEND
THROUGHOUT THE YEARS

Preface

The Greece that the tourist usually sees is the Greece of the Parthenon and the Acropolis, of clear sunshine, bright seas, and of warm, friendly people. Rarely in the early 1960s did the tourist—or anyone else—recognize this idyllic land as a country on the verge of political upheaval. Then, as on our many earlier visits, we started out as such tourists. Beginning considerably before World War II we toured the country, guidebook in hand, to trace its ancient ruins in their enduring splendor, but only by returning year after year and coming to know the Greeks in their daily lives and in their politics did we begin to sense the Greece which is more than the remains of bygone greatness.

Gradually we came to see it as a country of basic contradictions. In many ways it was a developing nation emerging from a past of poverty and successfully facing its economic problems in the world of the 1950s and 1960s; in other ways, it was deeply troubled, at one and the same time looking forward economically and backward politically. Equipped only with a great love for the country and its outgoing and hospitable people, a love which grew greater as our work progressed, and a desire to learn some of the reasons modern Greece has so often been plagued by political turmoil, we ventured into this study. This book is the result of our quest.

In midstream of our endeavor, Greece was overwhelmed

by the upheaval which began with the crisis between king and prime minister in July of 1965, and ended with the eclipse of constitutional representative government in April 1967. The suddenness and violence of the final change brought back the memory of earlier coups and stressed the many underlying causes for sudden shifts in the political life of modern Greece. We have tried to explore the factors in the Greek background which have contributed to this lack of stability. This book makes no pretense whatsoever of adding to the sum total of knowledge of Greek history, which we have emphasized merely to point up its part in causing the problems of the present. The reader therefore will not find the depth of detail or all the necessary caveats which scholarly historical writing requires.

We have tried, however, in the words of Thucydides, "to proceed upon the clearest data," and "to avoid partiality for one side or the other." In dealing with bitterly controversial political developments, the impact of which has not yet been softened by time, we have not presumed to pass judgment on the issues. We have adhered rigorously to a cut-off date of April 21, 1967, and so have discussed only the causes leading up to the coup of that day but not the form of government, the events, or the personalities involved after that fateful date. Above all, we have not attempted to read the future in a land where past oracles predicted the future only in riddles. The riddles might well be greater today.

Our focus has been on Greece itself rather than on Greece in its relations with the rest of the world. Thus the country's international affairs, its relations with its neighbors, and especially those concerning the tragic island of Cyprus, although they gravely concern Greece's development, are not discussed in critical detail.

Source material for the volume is indicated, wherever possible, in notes at the end of the book. We have also appended a bibliography selected from the constantly increasing number of works on modern Greece which have appeared in English. Lack of space has prevented listing the many important publications in other languages, although two or three exceptions in French and German have been noted. But our most valued sources cannot, unfortunately, be documented. On many different occasions in various years ending in mid-March 1967, when the country was preparing for elections which were never held, we talked to many people, reflecting various facets of Greek life. In cities, in towns, on farms of mountain and plain, we conversed with people from differing walks of life—statesmen and civil servants, shopkeepers, business and professional men, craftsmen, farmers, teachers, and housewives. Our thanks are given to all; without the insights they provided, this book would not have been possible. We should also like to thank our many friends in Greece and in the United States who have been generous with their wisdom and their knowledge and have given us wise criticism and deep understanding. We must reluctantly thank them only collectively.

Where Greek proper names are not unduly dissimilar to the English, we have kept the Greek, as, for instance, in the name of the northern Macedonian city of Thessaloniki. In using that form rather than the English name of Salonica, we have followed the practice of the United States Department of State. In transliterating Greek words, we have tried to approximate their sound and not necessarily their spelling in Greek. For instance, we have spelled Karamanlis with the letter *k* and have written Zakhariades instead of Zachariades, Chalkidiki rather than Chalcidice, and Kykládes instead of

Cyclades, all for reasons of Greek pronunciation. Where the use of *k* would make a name well known in English, such as Constantine, appear ridiculous, we have kept the *c*.

We have proceeded on one basic hypothesis—that for all its political upheaval, Greece will eventually find a way to solve its sorely besetting problems. We are convinced that Greece, in many ways responsible for the origins of what is finest in Western democratic traditions, and even for the word democracy, will again work out a democratic and constitutional form for its government. The ancient and the modern history of Greece and the freedom-loving Greek people have repeatedly shown that they have "an invincible power to survive internal strife."

Jane Perry Clark Carey
Andrew Galbraith Carey

L'Alberone
Weston, Connecticut
March 1968

Contents

The Web of Modern Greek Politics

CHAPTER 1

The Setting

In the early morning hours of April 21, 1967, tanks of the Greek army moved into position in front of the Parliament building in Athens' Constitution Square. Other key buildings and areas were similarly and promptly surrounded and occupied, and leading political figures were arrested. In a bloodless coup, and in a matter of hours, the government of Greece was firmly in the hands of a military junta of two colonels and a brigadier general, and the king was virtually commanded by the troops of whom he was commander-in-chief.

Soon the nation's form of constitutional parliamentary government, *Vassilevoméni Dimokratia,* or democracy headed by a king, as the Greeks referred to it, had all but disappeared. The constitution of 1952, in effect until the coup, was no longer thought of as the embodiment of the public will, and key sections were abolished. Parliamentary elections, called for May 28 of that year, were abandoned, and the institution of a parliament was wiped out; the political party furthest to the left, dominated by but not entirely made up of Communists, was banned; members of other parties were under suspicion—many had left the country, thousands were imprisoned or exiled to one of the numerous Greek islands which dot the Aegean and Ionian seas. In their early pronouncements the military junta set forth the reasons for their actions. They believed that Greek political life had become cancerous and that surgery of this drastic type was essential to prevent anarchy and the possibility of a Communist take-over of power.

Sudden shifts of power and changes in the form of government had taken place many times previously in the one hundred and forty years since Greece had become an independent nation. The state had been transformed from a republic to a monarchy in the early days of the new nation in 1832, and just less than a hundred years later, from a monarchy to a republic, and back again. Those changes came about by constitutional adoption of the differing forms of government, although they were indeed the result of strong pressures. Before World War II there had been several periods of dictatorship after take-over by military force; there had also been one four-year interval of dictatorial control by a general who had originally come into power through legal channels.

The seizures of power by the military had come about for various reasons, including their wish to lessen the autocratic actions of a king, and to set up a constitutional monarchy; to change the form of the state from a monarchy to a republic; and to break the frequent stalemates of political parties. The most common cause was the desire to bring about a republican form of government. In the various military assumptions of power of that prewar era, officers of the armed forces assumed the role of political manipulators, protectors, and advisers, and they alone made the decisions as to when political conditions were ripe for their sudden intervention. To many people in Greece, however, the officers of the military forces, of the army in particular, appeared as the only group able to take control of the country in a crisis and in the absence of strong political parties and a strong government. Like the Greek Orthodox Church, the armed forces had a nation-wide organization and a sense of the nation, generally more apparent among its younger than its older officers.

With the re-affirmation of the principle of a monarchy immediately after World War II, and the growing belief within the armed forces during the subsequent years that they were the especial guardians of the king, there was no attempt to change the form of government and set up a republic—although a suspected plot for this purpose was uncovered in the mid-1960s. In the years since the end of the guerrilla fighting in 1949, growing economic strength within the country and what was hoped would turn out to be long-range political stability also had contributed to the containment of power within political channels until the spring of 1967.

Governments in various countries have been overthrown because poverty or stagnation gave the people no hope for betterment of the conditions under which they lived. Although Greece had been a poor country from the earliest times so that "Hellas and Poverty had always been foster-sisters," as Herodotus had said in the fifth century B.C., economic conditions did not provide the reason for the various coups of Greece, and in particular not for the one of 1967. In the mid-1960s the country was probably as poor in natural resources and as barren of land as when Herodotus wrote. Throughout the intervening centuries, Greek poverty had been compounded by continuing erosion of the land so that it had become common to say: "When God finished making the world He had a sack of stones left and used them to make Greece." Invasions, occupations, political disturbances, and frequent wars had continued from time immemorial. The four years of World War II in Greece, followed by Communist attack and guerrilla fighting in 1945 and from 1946 until 1949, appeared to have completed the holocaust.

Despite its natural poverty and devastation by man, Greece rose phoenix-like from its ashes of 1949. Thanks to the hard work of its people and huge infusions of foreign aid— notably British and American—Greece downed the Communists. It also had put its house sufficiently in order by the late 1950s for economic development to have taken firm hold. By 1964 progress had been so great that the United States terminated its economic aid, while continuing its military assistance because of Greece's position in NATO.[1] With slightly less than one-fourth of the national income re-invested in its economy each year, Greece had attained a rate of economic progress higher than that of most Western European countries.[2] In 1962, for instance, when the Italian "miracle" was already in flower, Italy had the highest annual rate of economic growth in the Western World, 8 per cent; in that same year Greece's gross national product, with a later postwar start, had increased at the rate of 4.9 per cent, and from 1963 through 1966, it averaged over 8 per cent.[3] From one of the lowest standards of living in Europe at the end of World War II, the Greek per capita share of the gross national product averaged $390 in 1961, and by the end of 1966, $530. It was a marked increase but still well below the $800 to $2,500 of the more advanced industrial countries.

The signs of progress had become visible everywhere by the mid-1960s. New roads were cutting through the country. A steadily expanding national electric power network covered nearly all the countryside whereas only a decade before, electricity had been available only in the larger cities and towns. The fleet of Greek-owned merchant ships had become one of the largest in the world. New industries, many of size

and types new to Greece, had been established in the cities
where, little more than ten years before, practically all enterprises had been small, family owned, lacking technical skills
and managerial expertise, inefficiently operated, and with
high costs. Although still the common pattern of industry,
this type of enterprise had ceased to be all-pervasive.

In agriculture, as well as industry, changes were clearly
taking place. The plains were dotted with tractors instead
of nothing but the formerly omnipresent, weary donkeys.
The age-old traditional subsistence farming was slowly and
painfully beginning to change as new and improved farming
methods were gradually adopted, more fertilizers used, and
new crops introduced. It was already possible for fewer
workers to produce larger and more profitable crops. As a
result, the income of the farmers was rising and they were
able to buy more goods on their trips to market.

Despite progress, there were deep-seated flaws in the economy which were responsible for considerable political unrest.
Greece still showed many characteristics common to poor and
developing countries striving to support large rural populations. Although a middle class had grown noticeably by the
mid-1960s, half the people still lived in small villages and
worked the land, but earned only one quarter of the national
income. Between the few rich and the numerous poor, and
between the employed workers in the cities and the impoverished peasant-farmers in the mountains or the fishermen of
the islands, sharp and bitter contrasts still persisted. Despite
the rapid growth of national income within less than two
decades, its distribution was highly unequal, among not only
different categories of people but also different regions of the
country. Even with the rise in farm earnings generally there
was great disparity between the income of a wealthy plains
farmer and one struggling with sparse and eroded mountain

soil. The greatest difference lay between the rise in the city dweller's standard of living and the farmer's. Farm earnings were rising proportionately much less than those in the cities, and so the disparity was growing greater.[4]

In the rural areas especially, many people were still entirely unemployed, worked only part time, or seasonally. Attracted by the prospect of work in the industries of the cities, or having learned that wages were higher in various other countries, especially in Western Europe, thousands of people were leaving the land just as they have done in other countries. In the early 1960s, the rate of emigration had risen so much that it exceeded the natural growth of population and drained Greece of all too many of its youth.

Agriculture had undergone few structural changes. Little progress had been made in consolidating the tiny, separated plots into which so much of the farmland was divided, and the workers still had to spend weary hours in travel between their separated fields. In addition, the division of the land made it impossible to have the mechanization needed for efficient cultivation. The types of crops had not been changed sufficiently to meet Greece's modern needs, and, as in developing countries generally, there was still too much wheat, too little cotton and other cash crops, too little livestock and fodder. Too many goats ravaged the landscape and ate the shoots of the young trees, and there were not enough cattle to supply even domestic demand. Farm products constituted well over 80 per cent of Greece's exports but consisted chiefly of tobacco, currants, and raisins, all of which are subject to sudden and sharp changes in world tastes and prices.

The considerable economic growth of the country had been accounted for too largely by such investments as luxury housing instead of by projects which would increase Greece's wealth, and much of the capital used in the process of industrialization was foreign rather than Greek. The needs of new industries for imported machinery and raw materials, plus the demand of the city dwellers for more luxury goods from foreign countries, increased the deficit in the country's balance of payments. Even the growing receipts from shipping, from money sent home by Greek workers and emigrants abroad, and from the booming tourist trade, could not by themselves rectify the deficit.

The deeper reasons for the breakdown of parliamentary government in the spring of 1967 or in the earlier coups cannot be blamed on the poverty of the country, on its economy, or on any other single factor. The most sensitive difficulties of modern Greece have always been political and social, and they have deep roots. Explanation must be sought in many places: the sources of Greek government and its operation, the character and social mores of the Greeks, the geography and topography of their country, and above all their history.

The form of modern Greece's government was not selected in response to the country's own needs, interests, and aspirations, nor has it subsequently evolved toward them. During all Greece's lifetime as an independent nation, foreign ideas have permeated its constitutions, its monarchy, and its system of parliamentary government and public administration. When the governmental pattern was laid down in the early nineteenth century, the experience of the ancient Greek city-states gave a vague inspiration rather than a blueprint for construction. French models of the decade following the French Revolution provided the background and some of the form of the stillborn constitutions of the years of insurrection against Ottoman control, and of the first constitutional document of the new Greek state.

When a republic was selected as the first type of Greek government, its president was named primarily at the wish of Russia, who together with England and France formed the protecting powers for the new nation. When the republic was followed by a monarchy, the protecting powers were largely responsible for its form and for its first king, whom they brought from Bavaria without consulting the Greeks. During his reign, strong German influence in government and administration was added to French background. Despite the establishment of a legislative body in 1844, the country cannot be said to have had a constitutional parliamentary form of monarchy because the king continued as the real source of authority.

Through all future constitutions, German, French, and English influence may be traced, and after World War II, when American aid to Greece reached a high point, American influence was added to the others as can be seen in parts of the constitution of 1952. Greece, therefore, continued "to live under constitutions set up during early constitutional developments, always bearing the stamp of foreign patterns, but paying scant attention to changes which had meanwhile taken place in the respective countries. Greece has therefore never gone through the process of evolution of real political ideas."[5]

Despite the importance of French ideas in the constitutions of the emerging Greek nation, of all the protecting powers England left the strongest imprint on the form of Greek government by providing the model for its constitutional parliamentary monarchy established in 1864. But the evolution of constitutional provisions inevitably came about differently in the two countries. With its own traditions and way of life, Greece could not share the roots of a government indigenous to England and based on its own particular background and history. By the midnineteenth century, England had had centuries of political development uninterrupted by foreign invasions, and of long constitutional struggle which had strengthened the English concept of the rights of individuals in a free country. Greece, on the other hand, had a background of repeated foreign invasions and many centuries of foreign occupation.

From 1864 on, the years of Greek parliamentary life, although frequently interrupted, were spent in attempts to cut the standard pattern of English government to fit the Greek cloth; but concern centered on the pattern's exact fit rather than on possibilities for give and take at the seams to allow the model to be adapted. A pattern cut to suit English taste did not necessarily suit the Greek wearer even in 1864, and in the years up to 1967 form and detail as well as style were changing in Britain, while for most of the period Greece was struggling to adjust the import of 1864.

Even in Britain, where there is no one written constitution, progress came slowly. Although the monarchs of that country have become increasingly symbolic of the unity of the nation, they have been divorced from the exercise of political power only since the beginning of the twentieth century. It was not until after the death of Queen Victoria that the monarchs began to refrain "from any such measures of personal political partnership or of personal objection to appointments as Queen Victoria frequently exercised."[6]

Up to mid-1967, constitutional practice in Greece continued to allow the king to play a political role. In neither 1864 nor under later constitutional provisions pertaining to the monarchy and the government was the position of the king made entirely clear, and they no more than the statutes or the de-

velopment of constitutional practice prevented the crown
from taking part in politics. Constitutionally the king was
not an absolute monarch, nor was he merely the ceremonial
head of the nation, cutting ribbons at dedications of monu-
ments or public buildings. In other words, he neither ruled
nor reigned but did a little of both. Because the extent of the
crown's powers was never clear, they became the chief subject of political dispute over a long period of time and never
prevented the king from taking part in politics when he felt
occasion demanded.

During the centuries of foreign occupation Greece had little
opportunity to develop effective local self-government which
was basic to the growth and operation of the English parliamentary system. The House of Commons was composed of
members who often had previous experience in the small
units of English government, the shires and the counties.
The Greeks had little experience with self-government as a
training school for national service. They had developed
their own locally elected authorities, and under the Ottoman
occupation the need for administering a vast empire caused
the Ottoman government to turn over certain administrative
tasks to locally chosen Greek councils as well as to the Orthodox Church, which was itself organized on the basis of a
highly centralized hierarchy. In no sense did local government
or the Church provide any training ground for participation in the government of the Ottoman Empire. The Greeks
who rose in its service did so because of other background or
experience.

When the nation was formed, the Greek people had no
practice in local voluntary organizations of any kind which
would have helped ready them for work in representative
government and political party organization. Citizen groups,
each working for its own ends and each armed with a pro-

gram for action, have helped develop civic consciousness in England and the United States and have prevented frequent resort to revolutionary means of reform in those countries. Such groups were unknown in Greece, as in a number of other poor nations, where the place of voluntary organizations was filled by the strong and extended family and by deeply entrenched religious organization. The passage of time eroded their influence only slightly, and so even in the late 1960s they continue to do much of the work which might otherwise be carried on by voluntary organizations. Thus civic consciousness has been slow to develop.

In countries where representative government has worked comparatively well, the character of the national press has given strength to the political process. There was always freedom of the press in Greece, except in periods of dictatorship. As literacy became widespread among the Greeks, they read the papers and periodicals avidly. In late 1966, it was reliably reported that there were 127 newspapers in the country and that the city of Athens alone boasted 17 dailies and 43 weekly, semiweekly, biweekly, or monthly publications. Unfortunately, however, the large number merely reflected the many political currents and political parties. The press was the spokesman of political parties and of a few dominant families. It did not exist to present any conflict of interests, much less to present the news objectively. Its only aim was to win friends and influence people for the political parties and politicians who subsidized the papers. The press was so heavily involved in politics that many people became convinced that the Communist-controlled newspapers and journals, although subsidized from abroad, were the only ones not involved in political dishonesty within Greece. While the sheer number of papers and periodicals would appear to indicate that people in general were intrigued by the type of journalism the press presented, thinking citizens objected strongly to it as merely the paid voice of political parties. The papers were called by a leading Greek patriot "one of the worst features in the political life of Greece" and one of the chief reasons why representative government failed to develop along sound lines.

From its earliest days as a modern state, Greece has suffered from centralized government which keeps the citizens remote from its operation and fails to make them participants in the political process. As early as the coming of independence to Greece, the locally elected councils were grafted on the organs of the central government by the attachment to them of the *nomarchs* (prefects) appointed by it. Influenced as much by fear of the power of the separate local chieftains and by the wish to enhance their own power as by any desire to promote the unity of the nation, the *nomarchs* began to substitute central for the local initiative which had been exercised under Ottoman control. The *nomarchs* thus laid one of the foundation stones for the strong centralized control over local units of government which was to become so important a factor in the nation's administration in the years ahead and was to smooth the path for the various periods of dictatorship to come. Centralized administration in which the individual citizens were far removed from the seat of control was also a reason for lack of citizen participation in and understanding of government.

Although Byzantine and Ottoman traditions were not without influence, foreign patterns adopted by the new nation also helped lead it along the path of centralized administration. In its earliest years as a modern nation, Greece was deeply influenced by French ideas of centralized administration, and further centralizing tendencies were encouraged by the first king, a Bavarian, and by his ministers who had been trained in the centralized tradition of their native country. French and German administrative ideas continued to affect the Greek administrative structure throughout the nineteenth and early twentieth centuries. Administrative centralization finally reached such a peak under the dictatorship which lasted from 1936 until 1940 that the old system of local communal councils became moribund.

During and after World War II the sources of foreign administrative influence changed. Britain and the United States provided deliberate stimulus which gave the old local institutions new constitutional importance. But these never became strong enough to overcome the administrative domination of the central government. The formal political organization of villages and towns did not secure responsibility for even the affairs which were their especial concerns except in the most minor matters. For instance, village schools were supervised and controlled entirely by the Ministry of Education and Religion in Athens which even prescribed the curricula and appointed the teachers throughout the country.

The government in Athens controlled the purse strings of all local governmental activities except in the most infinitesimal affairs. Taxes were collected by the central government; budgets of local authorities and the *nomoi* were sent to Athens for approval; expenditure of funds authorized for even a small village was supervised in detail by the governor of the *nomos* in which it was located; and the governor in turn formed part of the Ministry of the Interior in Athens. These governors, the mayors of towns and cities, and even the locally elected officials had to stand obsequiously, hat in hand, if they wanted funds for even the most essential needs of their communities and regions. Whether or not they got what they needed depended entirely on personal relationships with higher officials. With only a vote in national elections and no other voice in anything except a limited number of their own immediate affairs and no way of financing their needs except through appeals to the central government, Greek villagers or townsmen, no matter how great their interest in politics, had little or no way to participate in public affairs.

The administrative arms of the central government tended to concentrate more and more political power in themselves. Within each ministry there was undue concentration of authority and work at the higher levels of government, in the ministers' offices, and in the capital city of Athens, from which all decisions radiated. With decisions left so much to overburdened ministers, the wheels of administration ground out their work at a snail's pace and so added to the existing cynicism concerning government, endemic in Greece since the days of foreign occupation.

Anyone visiting a minister's office in Athens in the mid-1960s was likely to find the office crowded with people awaiting decisions not only on matters of policy but on personal favors which the minister alone had the power to give, while members of the staff came and went, bearing papers to be signed. This activity was usually accompanied by noise of the constant thump of the stamping of documents of approval or disapproval, for a particular request. It was small wonder that the need for such approval or personal favor and the slow pace at which they were ground out led to the use of bribes in more than one instance, no matter what party was in control of the government.

The ways in which constitutional and political importations worked and the ways in which the public administration developed depended on Greek mores and traditions, the concept of *philotimo,* the role of the family and of the Church.

Philotimo refers to self-esteem and love of honor, and implies a deep-seated respect; it is not merely pride, which to the Greeks is tantamount to arrogance. Individuals, families, places of birth, and the nation all have their own *philotimo*. There is nothing a Greek will not do for anyone who appeals to his sense of it. Slight to the *philotimo,* or its molestation as the Greeks refer to it, constitutes a serious offense calling for retaliation. A Greek-born and Greek-educated student of these matters wrote: "A Greek addressed in a completely objective manner, on hearing his way of life described in harsh scientific terms, is greatly offended. A Greek presents each fact wrapped in some objective protective covering . . . if Greeks have to criticize, they do it with oratory also, reviling passionately. . . . The covering of the naked fact is essential to the integrity of the *philotimo.*"[7]

At the basis of the deep individualism of the Greeks, of their passionate love of freedom, and of their democratic character lies *philotimo.* It is a recognition of the value of an individual and of his right to his own freedom so that the Greeks do not think in terms of superiority or inferiority of one person as compared to another—although in Greece, as in the United States, attainment of business or commercial success inevitably brings welcome recognition. Except for brief interludes modern Greece has always been a monarchy, but the democratic nature of the Greeks may be seen, for instance, in the constitutional prohibition against the conferring or recognition of titles of nobility. There is no titled aristocracy, although families in the Ionian Islands, who had been granted titles by the Venetians during their long occupation of the islands, have been allowed to retain them for use informally at home but nowhere else in Greece. Similarly, various Phanariot Greek families (so-called from the Phanar quarter of Constantinople, near the Greek Patriarchate, where they originated) who ruled Christian provinces under the Ottoman Empire were given the hereditary title of Prince, but their descendants are forbidden to use it in Greece.[8]

Family *philotimo* has strong repercussions on politics and administration as well as on urban and industrial development. Although eroded by changing economic patterns and social custom, the family rather than the individual is still the basic unit of Greek society. In a family are included remote relatives such as second or third cousins and a *koumbara* or marriage sponsor, even though the latter is not usually a blood relative. The sense of this extended family is so strong that it affects all aspects of life. Even in the late 1960s, most businesses and industries are still family affairs. Greek emigrants abroad, to the second and sometimes third generations, still send their relatives at home such large amounts of money that altogether they bring enough foreign exchange into the country to form an important asset in the Greek balance of payments.

Because of family *philotimo,* a man employed in the city wants to enable his poor village relatives to find work there, and so he tries to secure jobs for them wherever he has the right connections, in industry, the service trades, and even in the civil service. Americans call it nepotism or the spoils system when the relatives of a man employed in government are given government positions at his request, but a Greek believes the arrangement is not only inevitable but also wise and necessary. He would be disloyal to his relatives if he did not find positions for them. A man's first loyalty is to his family and not to an impersonal concept of honesty or abstract ideal of justice. If he fails his family, he has offended its *philotimo.* Honesty refers to dealings with relatives or those whom a person has come to trust.

Centuries of poverty and of attempts to outwit the foreign occupying authorities have provided a background for distrust of those outside the family circle and in particular the government. In modern Greek life the highly centralized government and its representatives are too remote from people in their daily affairs to command loyalty or honesty. But especially in the 1960s, there has been a growing bitter resentment of corruption in the sense of money payment for favors granted or votes cast.

Although beginning to take a new role in society, Greek women and girls have their own particular type of *philotimo*. Soon after World War II and the ensuing guerrilla fighting, a number of outstanding university-educated women came to occupy high positions in public life, law, and government. Women were given the suffrage in 1952—although not allowed to use the right for four years—and city women soon became active. They had long been at work in the promotion of welfare organizations, particularly those concerned with maternal and child health and welfare.

Many women in the countryside, however, still occupy the role long assigned to them by tradition which effectively excludes them from politics. A peasant woman wields great authority in the home, where she is the dominant figure in relation to the children. The public life of the village has long been a male world, and a woman seldom if ever enters the strictly man's institution of the coffee house, not because she is considered inferior but because her appearance there indicates a lack of modesty. Similarly women seldom take part in the inevitable political discussions which enliven the men's hours in the coffee house and the *plateia* or village square.

As people moved to the cities in increasing numbers in the 1950s and 1960s, women began to take positions in the service trades and even in government. Women industrial recruits at first were frowned on, as they had been in the early industrial revolution in England, but their new role gradually became common enough to be accepted as being without stigma. An entering wedge into the system was provided by the need for women to earn money to help build up their dowries.

Next in importance to the family in molding the Greek character is the Greek Orthodox Church.[9] Practically all people adhere to the Church for the simple reason that they are Greeks and it is Greek. Ever since its split from the Roman Catholic Church in the eleventh century, the Orthodox Church has represented Greek values not only in spiritual heritage but also in culture, history, language, and education. Whether or not a Greek follows its dogmas closely, or has a high or low opinion of the priests, it is impossible for him not to feel a part of the Church. His education has always emphasized his religion, and elementary and secondary schools have been constitutionally required to provide an education aimed at the intellectual training and development "of the national consciousness of youth on the ideological principles of Greek Christian civilization."[10]

Although the first king of modern Greece never relinquished his Roman Catholicism, since 1844 the heirs to the throne and all subsequent monarchs have been required to profess the Orthodox faith as the established religion of the nation and an official part of the state under the constitutions. Eight years after the adoption of this requirement the Orthodox Church of Greece started on its own independent path when the Patriarch of Constantinople as the head of the Church grudgingly consented to the establishment of an autocephalous Greek Church on Greek soil. Since then the Patriarch has had only spiritual authority over the Church within Greece, and its affairs have been administered by the Archbishop of Athens, whose title as Archbishop of Athens and Primate of Greece indicates his authority. The fact that the Greek Church is the supreme authority in its own affairs has linked the people's feeling of pride in both Church and nation and bound them more closely to both.

Although he was the supreme authority of the state under the Constitution of 1952, the king did not control the Church. Symbolic of the Church-State relationship was the great midnight mass in Athens on Easter. The king, preceded by twenty-four pure white horses and followed by twenty-four bays, rode to the Cathedral where the Archbishop awaited. On the stroke of twelve the bells rang out the dawn of Easter, and the voice of the Archbishop called out, *Christos Anesti*: Christ is Risen. Although the king played an integral part in the ceremony, the dominant figure was the triple-crowned Archbishop.

A Greek's attachment extends beyond his family circle not only to the Church but also to the country and town of his birth. Thus local and national *philotimo* are of prime importance in government, politics and administration. A man's relationship to his town, section of the country, and nation is purely personal. The village from which he comes is a kind of extension of his already large, extended family, and his province and nation are still further extensions. The people from the same village who have migrated to a city look after each other, unless there has been a feud between them. Hundreds, perhaps thousands, of native sons have made fortunes abroad and then returned home to build schools or hospitals in their native villages. The Greeks are immensely proud of their nation and are willing to fight with the utmost courage and to die for it in time of war, but in peace time the *philotimo* of their nation seldom implies any sense of impersonal loyalty to an institution broader than the family. The lack of civic training and experience in voluntary organizations help account for this. Hence national like local politics remains personal.

Despite their cynicism about government generally, the Greeks have an unrivaled passion for politics. The mere mention of the word *politiki*—derived from *polis*, the Greek word for city—starts the Greeks on a long line of discussion, as happened, for instance, when the authors were in a remote and poor mountain village of Arcadia in the Peloponnese. As always in such cases, our arrival was heralded by a gathering in the local coffee house of the men of prominence, the notables of the village, including the mayor and schoolmaster, with those of lesser importance, in immaculate and much-patched clothing, crowded in the background. As we talked of the difficulty of finding work in that isolated spot being the chief reason the men were leaving the village, those on the fringes listened interestedly. But when we mentioned the English word *politics,* so nearly like the *politiki* from which it is derived, the silent men from the back of the room suddenly crowded close and began to take an avid part in the discussion.

Before we really settled down to talk of Greek politics, one of the men of that remote village began the conversation by expressing his sympathy to us as Americans for the sinking a few days previously of the submarine *Thrasher* with its attendant loss of many American lives. There is no television in Greece, but every village has at least one radio, and newspapers are read by the far from illiterate population.

The roots of this interest in politics go far back into Greek psychology as well as history. Psychologically, one of its origins lies in Greek love of talk and argument, *couvenda,* a kind of conversational matching of wits, carried on for sheer pleasure. This may well have originated in the isolated ancient Greek communities, where the people were thrown back on each other for interest and amusement. In ancient Greece the art of the dialogue first developed. In the Greece of those days one of the duties of a citizen was to learn to talk in public and express himself well in doing so. But the concept of a citizen included more, and the person who failed to take a part in the life of his community was referred to as *idiotes*, the useless man.

An all-important part of the national *philotimo* of the Greeks is found in an interest in their history and a spirit of national pride in the greatness of their past as the fountainhead of Western culture and civilization. An indelible mark was left on the thought and life of Greece by the world of mythology revealed by its ancient literature and by modern archeology. Greek roots are sunk deep in the Homeric poets and their ideals, the essence of which was "a dynamic conviction of the worth of the individual, which motivated a restless desire for excellence in every department."[11] The ancient city-states provided further inspiration. Of the early influences, those of the Byzantine Empire furnished the strongest and most continuing source of nourishment for the Greek sense of pride in their past. The War of Independence from 1821 to 1827 showed the determination of the Greeks to be free, to live a life of their own based on the proud traditions of their past, untrammeled by foreign occupation. Approximately the first hundred years of Greek national life were spent in attempts to bring all of those of Greek background into one nation as the Greeks had been in the wide-stretching Byzantine Empire. The four years of Axis domination, from 1940 to 1944, followed by the years of guerrilla fighting until 1949, once more renewed the sense of the Greek desire for freedom and their own continuing life, despite what appeared to be insuperable odds. The struggle over Cyprus again made them aware of their belief in the essential unity of the Greeks, but it was always their great past to which they turned for inspiration and help.

CHAPTER 2

The People and Their Background

In no country more than Greece have geography, topography, and history been so intertwined with the composition of the people and their political fate. A rugged and harsh land of some 51,000 square miles, Greece is slightly smaller than the state of Illinois and almost exactly the size of England. Unlike England, Greece's territory is neither compact nor homogeneous and has always presented a formidable hurdle in the path of the country's unification.

Greece's past and present have borne the strong imprint of its geographic location in relation to Europe and the Middle East. The Greek mainland is an integral part of the European continent and juts out from the Balkans like a forearm and hand, with fingers that reach into the Mediterranean. The countless islands—local fishermen say there are 1,000—constitute a quarter of the land area of the whole country and dot the Ionian and Aegean Seas thickly. It was a short move for early migrating peoples to go from one island to another and for later invaders and pirates to attack them from the sea.

The seas around Greece have been its highway and have carried its destiny. Almost everywhere they penetrate the shores in deep, winding gulfs; bays alternate with straits and islands except on the comparatively smooth and unbroken northern coast of the mainland. Along the coast—Greece has the longest coastline in Europe—are found the numerous natural harbors which made Greece a country of seafarers before the days of the *Odyssey* and provided safe havens for invaders coming from other lands throughout many centuries. The harbors, strategically located for control of the Mediterranean, were coveted by various nations in the era when domination of the seas was the driving motive in international rivalry. Nor had the importance of those harbors ceased in the late 1960s, when it appeared that a new manifestation of Russia's age-old longing for warm water ports was coming to the fore again.

Instead of diminishing the strategic importance of Greece, air power increased it. In 1951 the Greek nation accepted an invitation to join the North Atlantic Treaty Organization (NATO) and a few years later found itself facing the rumored possibility of having nuclear missile bases within its territory.

Like the seas, the mountains have played an all-important part in Greek history and political development. From the air, the country, especially its islands, appears as a series of mountains sunk in the sea with only the highest peaks rising above its surface. This appearance is not deceptive as the mountains constitute two-thirds to three-quarters of all the land.

Until the age of airplane travel the mountain formation made communications difficult with the European continent and with the rest of Greece. Impassable heights often made it necessary for mainland Greeks to take to the sea to reach nearby places on the same mainland. While the seas pushed the people of Greece outward, the mountains hemmed them in and forced them to turn in upon themselves. Thus the mountains slowed up the process of Greek unification.

Long valleys run from north to south on the mainland and are separated from each other by desolate and forbidding ranges, which in turn are crossed by other mountains running irregularly east and west. The valleys are found only between the mountains, and the plains exist only between the mountains or along the coasts. What Homer sang of the Ionian Island of Ithaca applies to much of the land elsewhere in Greece: "We have no level runs or meadows, but highland, goat land. . . . Grasses and pasture land are hard to come by." Like the seas, the valleys through the mountains brought invaders and conquerors from time immemorial, and these gradually changed the composition of the Greek people and the pattern of their history. But in considerable part the invaders were culturally conquered by the country they had subjugated.

As a result of separation by mountains and seas, several different Greeces exist within the confines of the one small country. Each differs from the others in land, climate, and to a certain extent characteristics of the people. The mainland, with areas varying widely from north to south, and from mountain to plain, differs from the islands. They in turn differ greatly from each other, and the large ones, such as Corfu (Kerkyra), Crete, and Rhodes, have great differences within themselves.

Greece has always been a bridge for trade between west and east and from the north to the Mediterranean. It was inevitable that invasions would sweep back and forth across this country. Some, like the Persians in the fifth century B.C., were repulsed; others, like the Romans, succeeded in overcoming Greek resistance. Later the Slavs, flooding southward through the mountain passes, were almost completely assimilated by the Greeks. Of the later occupations, Venice held a considerable part of the Greek mainland and islands for over six hundred years and left the deepest imprint on life and institutions in places such as Crete where Venetian control lasted longest. During the last centuries of the occupation by Venice, before it was finally expelled by the advancing Ottoman Empire, control alternated between the two in a number of places. Between them, practically all of what is now modern Greece had been dominated by a foreign power at one time or another, and occupations lasted from early in the thirteenth century until almost the mid-twentieth century.

With the emergence of the modern nation-states, the struggle for control of the seas and of the routes between Europe and Africa and Europe and the East made Greece an important pawn. The difficulties of the country were enhanced by its proximity to the nations and the peoples of the Balkans and of Turkey, all uneasy neighbors. After wars with Balkan countries and with Turkey, Greece was sucked into World War I. But it was World War II which again showed the importance of Greece's strategic location when the country was invaded by Italy, Germany, and Bulgaria before the Allied powers liberated the Greeks from Axis control. During that war, in the words of Winston Churchill, "the spasms of Greece . . . stood at the nerve center of power, law and freedom in the Western World."[1]

By the end of World War II there was a new element in the picture. Greece's northern neighbors, Albania, Yugoslavia, and Bulgaria, had fallen under Communist control, and all were anxious to extend their influence within Greek confines. In these countries were trained guerrilla fighters who came down to push the cause of Communism in Greece. In the struggle with the Communists, which lasted through years of fierce and bitter fighting in 1945 and from 1946 until the end of 1949, most Greeks were left with an ineradicable fear of warfare and especially of Communism. This fear was destined to leave a profound imprint on their political life in the years to come.

The Origins of the Ancient Greeks

The strategically located lands of Greece, its islands, and the neighboring coasts brought forth a people who were able to mold the great civilization of the fifth century B.C. in Greece. Long before that, perhaps in the sixth or fifth millenium B.C., a stone age people lived on the central plains of the Greek mainland and on the far-southern island of Crete, but little is known of them. From earliest times invaders and conquerers had entered the mainland from the long seacoasts or through the mountain passes and then used the islands as stepping stones. During the last few decades archeological evidence has made it appear that a migration of peoples westwards from Asia Minor to Greece took place long before people came south through the mountain passes into what is now Greece. These people, from east as well as north, mixed with the original inhabitants to form an early amalgam.

Names such as Ionian or Aeolian appear in early Greek history, but it is not clear whence came the bearers of those names, who the people were, or why they should be thought of as entirely Greek. Apparently they originated in the north of the Greek mainland and may have been driven south by another people, the Achaeans, who about the beginning of the second millenium B.C. came down through the valleys of northern Greece.

A branch of the Achaeans developed into the Myceneans, who in turn were strongly influenced by the Minoans of Crete, who themselves became the architects of another great civilization. In about 1200 B.C. the Myceneans laid siege to Troy: this successful siege and the ensuing adventures of the victors were sung by Homer in the *Iliad* and the *Odyssey* in about the eighth century B.C. Apparently depleted in vigor and wealth by the Trojan wars, the Myceneans declined rapidly thereafter, and soon they and the rest of the Achaeans disappeared.

According to some sources, about one hundred years after the siege of Troy, another people, the Dorians, possibly related to the Achaeans, began to come down into what is now Greece from the north. Driving Ionians and Aeolians ahead of them, the Dorians carried out the first devastating conquest of the country that was destined to be invaded and ravaged so often in the centuries ahead.

Bands of Achaeans, Ionians, Aeolians, and even the pursuing Dorians settled in the Aegean Islands and on the Aegean coast of Asia Minor, now part of Anatolian Turkey, little more than a stone's throw from the islands. Civilization in the area had existed long before any of the four groups reached there, and so they intermingled with the ancient inhabitants. As early as the eleventh century B.C. Smyrna, which is the city of Izmir in Turkey today, was settled by groups of people from the islands. About one hundred years later, on the coast to the south of Smyrna, numbers of Ionians, emigrating southwards from Attica to escape the Dorian onslaught, founded the city of Miletus. It became one of the great cultural and commercial cities of antiquity, and from it and other Ionian cities came some of the most illustrious names in ancient thought. By the ninth century B.C. the middle section of the Aegean coast of Asia Minor was controlled by various peoples whose ancestors in great part had come from the Greek mainland. From the name of the early settlers of the coast, the area came to be called Ionia. There appears to be no connection, however, between this name and that of the sea west of Greece, also called the Ionian.

Ionia was one of three parts into which the eastern

Aegean coast was divided. The Aeolians and the Dorians each controlled a section, with their own cities and their own types of political organization. Gradually the Aeolian people and their name faded away and only the Dorians were left to become serious rivals of the Ionians.

Modern Greece has deep roots in these powerful and important cities of the ancient world; the passage of the centuries brought other peoples to them and created an ever-growing amalgam of what had been Aeolian, Dorian, or Ionian. The cities and regions of the coast of Asia Minor never constituted one single organized Greek political system, and their culture became intermingled with that of other peoples. Throughout the centuries, nevertheless, the coastal regions and particularly the cities were regarded as part of the Greek homeland, both by Greeks from the Greek mainland and by a large part of the population of the coastal cities themselves. By the early twentieth century, they had so large an ethnic Greek population and such a feeling of unity with Greece that they were a leading cause of war between Greece and Turkey from 1919–1922. After the defeat of the Greek armies in 1922 the Greek population was forced to flee, although some of their ancestors had lived on the Aegean coast for possibly eleven centuries before Christ.

People of the Ancient Colonies

Soon after the sixth century B.C. various of the Greek settlements on the Aegean coast themselves began to send out colonies and to found other cities. It was said that the seafarers of Miletus founded more than any other classical city, perhaps as many as eighty, stretching from the Atlantic and the Mediterranean shores of Africa to the Black Sea.

Along the Mediterranean coasts also stretched many colonies established by the cities of mainland Greece and by the islands. To the north the colonies extended along the coasts of Macedonia, Thrace, the Dardanelles, and far up the shores of the Black Sea. Today the ruins of the coastal city of Histria in Romania, for instance, testify to its ancient Greek greatness. To the south the ruins of colonies such as Apollonia and Cyrene on the coast of Cyrenaica in modern Libya tell the same story. Although there were colonies along the coast of Spain to the west, the most influential ones, established by the second half of the eighth century B.C., dotted the southern mainland of Italy and the island of Sicily. This group formed the most important part of *Magna Graecia* of the ancient world. Today the ruined temples of Paestum, south of Naples, and of Segesta and Agrigento in Sicily bear mute witness to the heights attained by the architecture of these colonies, where lived some of the greatest artists and scholars of ancient Greece. Large modern Italian cities, Syracuse, Taranto, Crotone, and others, for example, were Greek in origin.

In the colonies Greek commerce, craftsmanship, art, and philosophy took root. Speaking the same language and for the most part worshipping the same gods, the colonies remained constantly in close touch with the mother country. People of the colonies never forgot that they were representatives of Greek civilization. In the same way modern Greeks who have emigrated over the face of the globe have maintained close ties with their homeland.

Although the civilization of the northern Greek mainland had been bound up with that of the Balkans in ancient times, Greek colonies established along the northern coast and penetration into the area of Greeks from the south brought the influence of the city-states to bear in the north.

Early Greek Influences

With the rise of the emperors Philip II and his son Alexander the Great in the fourth century B.C., Greek influence spread still further. Both emperors were born in the Macedonian city of Pella, not far from Thessaloniki (Salonica), and were successive rulers of what became under them the great Macedonian Empire. After defeating Athens Alexander created the League of Corinth in 338 B.C., by which for the first time in its history Greece was unified. His empire itself was essentially Greek, and the language of the Macedonian court was Greek.

By founding colonies to the east and leading his followers to the banks of the Indus—not far from which he died— Alexander spread Greek influence far in that direction. Although his empire did not outlive him by many centuries, he had done much to forward the culture of Greece in other lands. The Persians achieved only partial and temporary control over a number of the Macedonian colonies, and even after Alexander's death Greek influence continued strong in the Middle East. There it formed a foundation for the Greek influence in the Byzantine Empire.

Conquest by the Romans

In the second century B.C. the Romans moved from their camps in what is now Romania and Yugoslavia and entered Greece through the northern valleys. They thus made Macedonia a stepping stone to their subsequent conquest of the rest of Greece. In 67 B.C., when they had overrun Crete in the southern seas and had captured a number of Macedonian colonies to the east, the Roman conquest of Greece had become complete. But in many ways the conquering Romans were themselves conquered culturally by Greece. After the sack of Athens in 86 B.C. by the Roman general Sulla, the influence of Greek art and literature penetrated Rome deeply. Sulla and later Romans shipped home much Greek sculpture which became the inspiration and model for a great deal of Roman art. The Romans kept Greek workshops busy making replicas for them, and Greek architecture had a marked influence on that of Rome. The Greek language became fashionable in Rome, and educated Romans sent their sons to Athens to study.

The Romans made Macedonia a center of trade and located their administrative headquarters for the area in Thessaloniki. For a long time southern Greece remained a Macedonian dependency as it had been under Alexander the Great. People and commerce moving back and forth brought continued southern influence to the north of Greece, and vice versa. Thessaloniki was the most important center of that influence. Its advantageous location at the crossroads of the southern Balkans and near the mouth of the Axios (Vardar) River gave the city a leading place in commerce. As the Roman administrative center for the area, it became an important post on the Via Egnatia (still used as the name of Thessaloniki's main street and of the modern ferry linking Italy and western Greece), which was the shortest land route from the Adriatic to Byzantium.

As a Roman province under the name of Achaea (to distinguish it from Macedonia), Greece enjoyed the benefits of the *pax romana* after the end of the Roman civil wars. But the Greeks supplied few recruits to the Roman army and apparently retained too much local interest to enter Roman official careers in any numbers.

The signs of change were apparent in the fourth century. The spread of Christianity caused the gradual closing of Greek temples dedicated to the old gods and brought about the end of the Olympic games. Meanwhile barbarian invasions had begun, at least sporadically and in 395, Alaric and his Goths entered Greece. That same year the Roman Empire was divided into the eastern and western parts and the star of the Roman Empire in the west was already setting.

Greeks and Hellenes

When the Romans first came into contact with the Greeks, the Greeks had no common name. It was apparently accident which gave them not only one name but two, *Greeks* and *Hellenes.* The Hellenes were one of the early tribes who had moved southward from the north of Greece; the *Graii,* a word which in Roman mouths became *Graeci,* was the name of another tribe stemming from the central part of the country. "The west got its 'Greece' from an obscure district in Boeotia; Greece itself got its 'Hellas' from a small territory in Thessaly."[2] The word *Hellenes* was possibly first applied to Greek colonists in southern Italy who became successful traders. They were proud of the name *Hellenes,* which their neighbors in that area gave them.

Later the people of Byzantium, calling themselves *Romaioi,* reserved the word *Hellene* for their language and as the name for a pagan rather than a Christian Greek. Gradually, in the early Middle Ages, the intellectuals of Constantinople, and more especially of Thessaloniki, conscious of their Greek heritage, began to refer to their "community of Hellas." By the end of the fourteenth century the Byzantine emperor was often called "Emperor of the Hellenes."

The Byzantine Empire

The guiding spirit in the founding of the Byzantine Empire had been Greek. Before the midseventh century B.C. the Dorian city of Megara on the Greek mainland had planted a group of colonies at the eastern end of the Propontis (Sea of Marmara) in what is now Turkey. Among them was Byzantium, located at the entrance to the Bosphorus, which leads from the Propontis to the Black Sea. Commanding the trade of these waters, Byzantium soon rose in commercial and political power and was destined to be the chief city of the Empire. The importance of Byzantium's location, however, was not fully realized until the metropolis became the rival and then the successor of Rome. Long referred to officially as "New Rome," the city was rechristened Constantinople in honor of the Emperor Constantine I, who was called the second founder of the city.

From the date of Constantine's coronation in A.D. 325, the Empire lasted over a thousand years, and for many of those centuries Constantinople was its proud and magnificent capital. It, rather than Athens, was the military, political, and economic heart of the Empire, the seat of the Greek Orthodox religion and of its Patriarch, the center of Greek thought and of Greek intellectual life.

Beginning about the eleventh century, and continuing for some three hundred years, the Empire slowly disintegrated, and in the process came the gradual decline of Constantinople until it was a melancholy, dying city. Its scholars grew ever more poverty-stricken and down-at-the-heel, but even through the later years of the city's material decline they continued their brilliant productive life. As their prosperity decreased, the scholars became increasingly more immersed in the greatness of their Greek background. When many fled, or were summoned to teach in Italy or elsewhere in western Europe, they carried with them a culture, knowledge, and philosophy definitely Greek in origin. The seeds they planted in the West grew into some of the finest flowers of the Renaissance.

During the millenium of Byzantine power, Thessaloniki, the capital of Macedonia, had become second in importance only to Constantinople in culture and commerce. By the eighth century the city had already become one of the important ports in the Mediterranean. Later its scholars and clergy preserved and nurtured the Byzantine cultural inheritance through the years of Ottoman occupation. Even today the mosaics of a church such as St. George (originally a Roman mausoleum) still bear witness to the city's Byzantine greatness.

Byzantine influence remained elsewhere in what is now the Greek nation, and fortified cities in Macedonia and Epirus kept the traditions of Byzantine culture alive through the later centuries of invasion and occupation. For many years the court of Arta on the mainland in far-western Epirus served as a refuge for people of Hellenic background fleeing from invaders coming with or following the crusaders from the west who were intent on the capture of Constantinople.

Not far from Thessaloniki, on the third and northernmost prong of the Chalkidiki peninsula, a Byzantine influence today continues to be of artistic importance and minor political interest. Mount Athos, the Holy Mountain, has provided a retreat into the past since the tenth century. Occupying a special place under the Greek constitution, Mount Athos contains a self-governing republic of monks, ruled by a council composed of one representative from each of the twenty Byzantine monasteries still located on its rocky heights. Today, amid crumbling masterpieces of its Byzantine past, a declining number of monks and hermits continue to live out their secluded lives, isolated from all female life, whether hens, nanny goats, or women.

Centuries of Invasion

While Constantinople and its eastern territories had grown strong during the early centuries of Byzantine power, the islands and mainland of Greece had suffered pirates from the sea and sporadic invasion by Goths and Huns who came down through the passes in the northern mountains. Although the star of its ancient greatness had already set, Athens in important part was destroyed by the invading Goths in the third century.

From the seventh century onward, the sea had borne Arabs to harass and raid the islands and part of the mainland. Continuing to make inroads for many generations, the Arabs went to Greece for booty, and except in the island of Crete did not establish themselves as permanent settlers. They took over Crete during the first quarter of the ninth century and continued to control it for well over one hundred years, founding the Cretan city of Khandeh, which came to be called Candia, now Iraklion or Heraklion.

The Slavic Invasion

A southward movement of the Slavs through the northern mountain valleys formed the great invasion of the early Christian era. In about the third century they began their trek from north of the Danube River, and within four centuries the full tide of Slavic invasion had inundated the Macedonian peninsula, driving the Greeks to the Aegean shores and pushing those who had become Latinized into the mountains of the north.

The original Slavs were joined by another Slavic group, the Bulgars. Originating on the Asiatic steppes and coming to Greece from the Black Sea area, the Bulgars entered the country in large numbers, beginning about the seventh century. Although they penetrated as far south as Corinth, for the most part they settled in Macedonia and Thrace. Since much of the countryside was already inhabited by large numbers of Slavs, the two groups first collided and then intermingled. From the eighth to the thirteenth centuries the Byzantine emperors tried to check the influence of the Slavs and Bulgars by bringing in different tribes of colonists from around the Black Sea.

Eventually the Slavic peoples so saturated Greece that its mainland was often referred to as *Sclavinia*. But Greek vitality and power of absorption were so great that they ultimately engulfed the Slavs and converted them to the Greek form of Christianity. Despite the size of the Slavic invasion, it left little mark on the country other than some place names, especially in the Peloponnese, and a few round heads and faces, characteristics believed by a few anthropologists to be particularly Slavic.

Centuries of Venetian Occupation

With the Byzantine Empire weakening and raiding Arabs wandering the seas, the Serene Republic of Venice began to reach out for power in the eastern part of the Mediterranean. By the beginning of the thirteenth century Venice had already achieved a considerable measure of success. Forgetting the avowed aim of the crusades to rescue the Holy Sepulchre in Jerusalem from "the infidel," the Venetians led the Fourth

Crusade on a detour to Constantinople, a detour which turned out to last for several centuries. In 1204 the city fell before the onslaughts of the crusaders, Venetians, Franks, and a group of assorted western Europeans. Constantinople and the Byzantine Empire as a whole were divided as trophies for the victors, many of whom remained in Greece to enjoy their prizes.

When the Empire and the city of Constantinople were partitioned among the conquerors, the Byzantine Empire was already in its death throes. Although it recuperated sufficiently to live on in the Peloponnese some two hundred years more, its strength and vitality had ebbed away.

In the division of 1204, under the flag of the Lion of St. Mark, Venice secured the lion's share of the city, a number of Aegean islands, and various strategic coastal points and ports of the Peloponnese.

Crete

In the same year as the partition Venice *bought* what came to be one of its most important possessions, the island of Crete, long a coveted prize. According to Homer, "amidst the dark blue sea, there lies a land called Crete, a rich and lovely island, washed by the waves on every side, populous beyond compute, and boasting ninety cities." Whether the island still had as many cities as that when Venice bought it in the thirteenth century is doubtful, but at least it was rich and strategically located. It was the fourth largest in the Mediterranean and was located sixty miles south of the Greek mainland, almost equidistant from Europe, Asia, and Africa.

Other countries had found its riches before the Venetians. With its great Minoan civilization, older than that of mainland Greece, Crete had become a world power by the mid-sixteenth century B.C. During the Roman era Crete had been incorporated into the Roman province of Cyrenaica in North Africa, of which it remained part until included in the Byzantine Empire in the fourth century. Constantly invaded from the surrounding seas, Crete was only temporarily lost by the Byzantines to the Arabs; it was regained and remained part of the Byzantine Empire until the partition of 1204.

In that year the island fell to the lot of Boniface, Marquis of Montferrat, leader of the crusaders, and it was he who sold it to the Venetians, who for over four centuries continued to rule it. Candia (Iraklion or Heraklion) became a Venice-oriented city, as still witnessed today by the Venetian fortress in the harbor with its great bastions emblazoned with the Lion of St. Mark, and the fountain of the Doge Morosini in the main square.

Crete developed a prosperous commerce under the Venetians, as did many of the islands and mainland ports under their domination. But Venetian control was too arbitrary for the freedom-loving Cretans. Some became so restive that they reportedly wished to exchange Venetian for Ottoman control.[3]

From Crete as from the Serene Republic itself, the Venetians had extended their influence and their commercial domination in the eastern Mediterranean to include places of which they were not in actual possession. Jealousy was the inevitable result, and Venice became engaged in contest with the Genoese, and then with the Ottomans for control of the mainland of Greece, the islands, and the coast of Asia Minor.

The Franks

Accompanying the Venetians on the Fourth Crusade had been various Frankish princes from western Europe. Many of them succumbed to the spoils, sun, climate, and pleasant way of life in Greece while others, for reasons best known to themselves, were anxious to stay away from Europe. The Franks established themselves, together with their feudal system, their jousts, and their tourneys, in various places throughout Greece. Achaia, for instance, a section of the Peloponnese, became a bit of France transplanted to Greek soil, where ruined castles stand today as silent witnesses to former Frankish power.

Under the Franks Athens was turned into a French duchy. In the early thirteenth century a Burgundian, Otho de la Roche, became the first feudal lord of Athens and Boeotia, with "the Acropolis for his castle and the Parthenon for his minster."[4] In 1260 his successor, Guy de la Roche, was created Duke of Athens by King Louis IX, St. Louis of France.

The French found Athens a poor and run-down city which had declined for centuries under the impact of one invasion after another and from long neglect. When cultural life had been transferred to Constantinople as the seat of Byzantine power, Athens continued to be a small town of only local importance. Whatever the Franks did to make the city French did not last long.

After a century of French rule, Athens was freed from its Frankish overlords, only to be overrun for another hundred years by marauding bands of Catalan mercenaries and adventurers. Afterward the city became successively Florentine, again Frankish, and Venetian before it finally succumbed to the Ottomans.

Meanwhile, in a last burst of strength the Byzantines had driven the Franks from the Peloponnese by 1432. But on both mainland and islands Venice had become the great colonial power.

Brief Stay of the Genoese

The Genoese had taken no part in the Fourth Crusade but soon after the midthirteenth century were called on by the weakened Byzantines to help drive the powerful Venetians from Constantinople, where after 1204 they had become deeply entrenched. In return for their help to the Byzantines, the Genoese received the wealthy city of Smyrna on the Anatolian coast, and Pera (Galata) on the mainland across the narrow waters of the Golden Horn from Constantinople.

Within a short time various Aegean islands fell to the Genoese—Chios, Lesbos, Lemnos, Thasos, and other smaller ones. These islands were so strategically located close to the Anatolian coast that they became the object of intense struggle. Lesbos, Samos, and Chios are merely continuations of the mountain ridges of Turkey. Lesbos, nestling in the crook of the Anatolian coast, and Samos, farther south, are so close to the shore that they seem part of it. Samos, for instance, is separated from the coast by a strait less than a mile and a half wide. The Anatolian mountains, like the Ottoman shadow, loomed over these islands and the Dodecanese to the south.

A particular bone of contention was the island of Rhodes, eleven miles from the Ottoman coast and close to the other islands of the Venetian-controlled Dodecanese. Located on the main sea path between Constantinople and Alexandria, Rhodes lay in the direct path of migrations from ancient Greece to Asia Minor, and straddled the routes of early trade. As a lush and green prize, cooled by the *meltemi*—the Etesian winds of the ancient Greeks—Rhodes had been repeatedly plundered by the Arabs, most notably in the seventh century.

In the final dispute neither Venice nor Genoa secured the

island. The Knights of St. John, retreating from the Holy Land via an eighteen-year sojourn in Cyprus,[5] reached Rhodes in 1309 and entrenched themselves there within sight of the neighboring Ottoman coast. In 1522, after a siege just short of five months, the Knights of St. John capitulated to the Ottomans, led by Suleiman the Magnificent, and withdrew to the island of Malta.

Centuries of Ottoman Occupation

Invited to Europe by a Byzantine emperor at the beginning of the fourteenth century to help ward off the threatening Serbs, the Ottomans defeated the enemy they had been summoned to fight and then, in the midfourteenth century, settled down on the European shores of the Dardanelles. Pushing rapidly westward through Thrace, they captured the important city of Adrianople in 1360 and moved their capital there from the green and watered city of Brusa (now called Bursa) in the mountains of Anatolia. From their new capital the Ottomans launched their campaign in which they hoped to conquer not only Greece but also all of southeastern Europe and ultimately western Europe as well.

Before the beginning of the fifteenth century the rich lands of Macedonia, and of Thessaly to its southeast, had been captured by the advancing Ottomans, and the great Byzantine city of Thessaloniki had been taken, probably in 1430 (there is doubt about the exact date), twenty-three years before the fall of Constantinople. As unsubdued in spirit by the Ottoman as by the earlier Slavic invaders, Thessaloniki retained the culture of Byzantium and remained the strong center of Hellenism, in communication with the other towns of southern and western Macedonia where Byzantine influence also remained great. In all of them the Orthodox clergy were the prime movers in keeping the Greek language and the Greek spirit alive.

From the fifteenth century on, one after another of the areas of Greece came under Ottoman control. Athens was captured in 1456, and, except for a few Venetian colonies on the coast, the large peninsula of the Peloponnese had everywhere been taken by the Ottomans within a few more years. After they had conquered almost all the Greek mainland and had captured a number of the Aegean islands, the Ottomans laid siege to Constantinople, still the capital of what was left of the Byzantine Empire. Despite the aid of courageous Venetian and other European allies, and the fourteen miles of heavily fortified walls which surrounded the city, the outnumbered and forlorn defenders could not withstand the strength of Sultan Mehmet's army of some 80,000 men.[6] Appeals to the Pope and to other sources of power in western Europe failed to bring help in time. When it came, it was too little and too late. In 1453 Constantine XI was killed in the battle, and the city surrendered to the Ottomans.

After the conquest Constantinople began a new era of prosperity and material well-being. The city remained the seat of the Patriarch of the Greek Orthodox Church and has continued as such. With the change of sovereignty in 1453 the art and culture of Greek Byzantium, which had persisted through good times and bad, withered away in the city. The Ottomans did not encourage learning among their Christian subjects, and the free spirit of the Greek heritage in Constantinople was largely submerged. But it had taken root in Rome, Florence, and Venice, where it was to grow and flower again in the Renaissance.

The location of the islands of the north and south Aegean so close to the Ottoman coast brought them one by one into

Ottoman hands. When the rich island of Chios fell in 1566, almost exactly three hundred years of Genoese importance in the Aegean came to an end. Within little more than one hundred years from the conquest of Constantinople, all the Greek mainland and all the Aegean islands had come into Ottoman control.

To the south, Venetian-occupied Crete still held out. Despite the bitter Cretan resentment of four centuries of control by the Venetians, Cretans and Venetians fought side by side defending Candia (Iraklion) in one of the long sieges of history, from 1648 until 1669. With the fall of the city, Ottoman conquest of Greece was complete.

During the more than four centuries of their control, the Ottomans followed a policy of using their foreign subjects to aid in the administration of the far-spreading empire. High offices in Constantinople were often filled by Greek Phanariots, many of whom became rich and powerful to the extent of being made princes over various Ottoman dominions. But the Phanariots remained a group apart, hated bitterly by the Greeks struggling to be free of foreign control.

Far more important, however, than the Phanariots' role was that of the Patriarch of Constantinople, who was given political control over the Greek Orthodox community. The Ottomans also expanded the powers of the old locally elected Greek councils, thus providing experience in "conditional self-government" for the Greeks. A financial contribution, for example, was demanded from each province. The collection was then turned over to the provincial Ottoman authorities, but they in turn often gave the local Greek communities responsibility for collecting their quota. How far control became local depended on the circumstances of individual Ottoman authorities. Much of continental Greece was held under tight rein from Constantinople because of chronic disturbance in the mountain and shepherd communities. In various places in the Peloponnese there was an extended hierarchy of Ottoman officials, but the local Greek councils frequently were strong enough to dominate them.

Preservation of the Greek Heritage

The closely knit Greek family system and the teachings and organization of the Greek Orthodox Church provided formidable forces in maintaining the spirit of the people and in perpetuating their culture and language as vital national links throughout the centuries of occupation. When the Franks controlled the country, they attempted to reunify the Greek and Roman Churches which had split bitterly apart in the eleventh century. The Franks also tried to establish Roman Catholic priests on Greek soil, but they failed in both attempts. Like their Frankish civilization, their religion left no lasting mark on Greek consciousness; the split between Eastern and Western churches continued, and the Greeks became steadily more tied to their own church. Although the Roman Catholicism of the Venetians made a more permanent impression, it was chiefly in the Ionians and the small Kykládes (Cyclades) groups of islands. As the centuries of Ottoman control passed, the Greeks drew steadily closer to their own church and to their own background.

The Greek Orthodox Church was the only Christian church not abolished by the Ottomans when they conquered Constantinople. After 1453 the titular head of their church, the Patriarch of Constantinople, was allowed to continue his residence there—as he still does—and was also made the political head of the Greek community. Thus he was responsible not only for the spiritual welfare of the Greeks but also for their political activities. He had important responsibilities for the administrative, financial, and judicial affairs of the "Romaic Nation," as the members of the Greek Orthodox Church were called. Because of his legal responsibility for his flock, he spoke for the Greeks in their dealings with the Ottoman authorities. So important were his political duties that the Patriarch's failure to prevent the outbreak of the Greek insurrection in 1821 meant, in Ottoman eyes, that he was unable to control the Greeks for whom he was held responsible; he and several of his assistants were executed two years later.

Under the Ottomans the temporal power of the Patriarch was always delegated downward through layers of lower ecclesiastical authority from archbishops to village priests. When, nearly thirty years after the new nation became independent, the Patriarch grudgingly consented to the establishment of the autocephalous church in Greece, the Archbishop of Athens became its head. As Archbishop of Athens and Primate of Greece, he became the presiding officer of the synod or administrative council of the Church of all Greece.

In the eighteenth century certain scholars condemned the Greek Church for what some of them called "its exhortation to resignation and acquiescence in Ottoman rule on the ground of the divine origin of all authority," which "retarded the intellectual progress and the political liberation of the Greek nation,"[7] but no one doubted that numerous Church dignitaries and especially local priests helped spark Greek resistance. Pride in the greatness of the Greek past and the dream of independence from foreign control had been kept alive continuously by the lower clergy and the village teachers, who sometimes were one and the same.

During those years a priest was frequently the only literate man in a Greek village, and he would often open a night school so that the boys might learn to read and write. By his teaching he was able to help preserve their ancient language and particularly to instill in his pupils a belief in the indestructibility of the Greek spirit. To some he appeared responsible for a backward rather than a forward look, but no one could deny his role in the maintenance of the Greek heritage.

The priests, together with the village headmen and teachers, were members of the elected councils of the villages. Although they carried out certain administrative functions, such as tax collection, as required by the Ottomans, they also resolved local disputes among the villagers. In the long run, however, the most important accomplishment of the councils was to help unite the people as Greeks.

In the latter part of the eighteenth century the importance of maintaining and ceaselessly renewing the Greek spirit was reaffirmed in the church and other quarters as well. A revival of interest in the scholarly study of the Greek past was brought about by a newly rich and important merchant and shipping class and a few powerful Phanariot Greeks. These prosperous groups founded a number of educational institutions and sent their teachers to western Europe for study of the Greek classics and philosophy. Original documents were better preserved there than in Greece, where they were subject to centuries of neglect and despoliation.

While abroad, many of the teachers became interested in the growing ideas of the Enlightenment and the French Revolution. On their return to Greece, they spurred their students to emulate the free spirit of their ancestors and to follow the call for liberty, equality, and especially for freedom. Among the chief admirers of the French revolutionary spirit was Constantine Rhigas, who founded *Hetairia,* an organization designed to encourage patriotism among the Greeks and even to provide them with arms for the coming struggle. Rhigas is remembered also for his translations of foreign works into popular Greek and for his revolutionary battle hymn. He was executed in 1798 for conspiring to bring about a Greek uprising and a popular government patterned on the French Constitution.

One of the chief ways in which the church and educational institutions transmitted the traditions of the past was by keeping the ancient language alive. But it was not a simple matter. Ancient Greek alone had consisted of four classical dialects rather than one uniform language, and so its teaching required considerable knowledge. With the passage of time, furthermore, variations had crept into the ancient language. As the influence of the Greeks in the ancient world spread abroad through colonization and trade, a variation called *Helleniki Koini* was developed. It used the most common existing Greek words but added others taken from the languages of different peoples in the Mediterranean basin. *Helleniki Koini* was the language in which the four Gospels and later the Greek liturgy were written and so came to be called "New Testament Greek." In a nation where the church has been as important as in Greece, this language was not unimportant in emphasizing the Christian background of the Greeks. As still more foreign words gradually came into Greek, the people's speech, called *demotiki,* began to differ considerably from both ancient Greek and *Helleniki Koini* and to lose some of its purely Greek character, particularly an ability to express abstract ideas.

To reform and purify the language and especially to help inspire and aid the struggle for political freedom, a scholar and translator of Greek classics, Adamantios Korais (Koraes), formulated an artificial language, called *katharévousa.* He was born in Smyrna in 1748 and so lived at a time when the forces for Greek independence were already beginning to exert themselves. *Katharévousa,* which went back to ancient Greek for inspiration, was based as much as possible on the syntax and vocabulary of the ancient language but was cleansed of subsequent additions from other languages. *Katharévousa,* referred to as "pure" or "purist" Greek, had great influence in promoting growth of the Greek national spirit during the last years of Ottoman control and the early years of independent Greece. The new language was to become the official one of the new Greece. But it was to be the spoken language of only those few who had learned it at school and even then only for official or formal occasions. Its usefulness was primarily patriotic, again to remind the Greeks of their great ancient past and their own link with it.

Birth of Modern Greece

Throughout the centuries of occupation, the spirit of the country remained intensely Greek. On the island of Crete and in the utterly isolated southern Peloponnesian peninsula of the Mani, the embers of freedom were kept especially warm. In Crete, as a crossroads of trade, Ottoman authorities appeared particularly numerous and oppressive, adding steadily to the burning Cretan wish for freedom from foreign control. The Mani, on the other hand, a rocky and waterless "landscape of pumice"[8] towered over and protected by the high Taygetus range, almost as high as snow-covered Mount Olympus in the north, is so isolated by nature that it was little touched by Ottoman influence. In the seventeenth century rebellion broke out among the people of this section, and when they were finally subdued by Ottoman power their submission was only nominal. High in their mountains, the Mani inhabitants bided their time until the insurrection of the early nineteenth century, when they became leaders in the fight for freedom. Even in the late 1960s, the people of the Mani, still isolated, and with many of their local customs unchanged, continue to live among the fiercely strong memories of their years of resistance.

In all other Greek lands and among all Greek peoples the desire to be masters of their own fate grew apace from the seventeenth to the nineteenth centuries. Everywhere the rumblings of insurrection became steadily more insistent. Under the Venetians attempts at revolt had been numerous, especially in Crete, but had been sporadic; under the Ottomans they had increased in number and violence. Even the top Greek clergy in Constantinople and many high-ranking Phanariots in Ottoman employ had begun to be restless.

After repulse at the walls of Vienna in 1683, the Ottoman attempt to conquer western Europe was abandoned, and the military strength and civil power of the empire disintegrated in a long, slow process. At it went on, pride and conviction that freedom was at hand rose higher and higher among the Greeks.

In the early nineteenth century, when Napoleon was still the dominating force in western Europe, and Russia was anxious to expand its power southward at the expense of the Ottoman Empire, both France and Russia sent agents to Greece to stimulate still further the existing spirit of disaffection. But they accomplished little. The Greek past remained the chief propelling force in the drive for freedom, and to it had been added the ideology of the French Revolution. Under the twin stimuli, Greek dreams of freedom began to take tangible form.

After the sporadic earlier uprisings in Greece, the first clear dawn of revolt against the Ottomans may be said to have come in 1821 in Wallachia and Moldavia in what is now

Romania. The seeds of revolution had been planted even deeper in Greek soil, and the people were ripe for action. In April 1821, when the blue and white flag of Greek independence was hoisted at the monastery of Aghia Lavra at Kalavryta in the Peloponnese, and when, soon thereafter, a similar signal was raised on the island of Crete, revolt got under way. In the same year, in the north, in the Epirot capital of Ioannina, the rebellion of the Albanian governor in Ottoman employ lit another beacon.

Fighting was carried on throughout the Greek mainland from 1821 until 1827. The cause of independence summoned not only Greeks but philhellenes from Europe and America to join the Greek cause. Throughout the years of revolt, the Greeks disagreed among themselves as to what form the government of their country should take, and how it should best be organized. With no national government experience behind them, such disagreement was inevitable. They had lived under occupying powers for over six hundred years.

In July 1827, after the Greeks had appealed to them, England, France, and Russia agreed to act as mediators, but favorable to the Greeks, in an attempt to end the struggle. That same month, by the Treaty of London, a small independent Greece was set up. In October of that year the combined fleets of the three powers, taking a somewhat equivocal part in the Battle of Navarino, helped deal the lethal blow to Ottoman power in Greece by destroying Turkish and Egyptian ships. Greece was free from occupation, but still under foreign tutelage.

CHAPTER 3

Growth of the Nation

The struggle for independence and nationhood in Greece was long and costly in effort and aroused violent national emotions. For many years it absorbed so much of the Greek vitality that it prevented the new nation from emphasizing the needs of its economic and political development. Instead, every energy was bent to the fight for freedom and then to the goal of enlarging the nation in territory and population so that expansion became the chief focus of politics. As Greece's frontiers became longer they required an increase in armies and thus in cost. These in themselves occupied so much of the political arena that development of the country continued to be regarded as less important than additions of territory.

Modern Greece as Originally Constituted

The new nation was small in both area and population. It consisted only of Central Greece, the Peloponnese, and the Aegean Islands of the Kykládes, a total territory approximately one-third of its present size. The northern frontier ran from the Gulf of Arta (Ambracian Gulf) of Epirus on the Ionian Sea eastward to the Gulf of Volos in Thessaly on the Aegean Sea. The northern shore of both gulfs and all the fertile provinces to the north in what is now Macedonia and Thessaly remained in Ottoman control. On the south the boundary was formed by the seas washing the mainland shores; the passionately Greek island of Crete was not included. To the east most of the Aegean Islands remained in Ottoman hands. To the west the Ionian Islands were controlled by the English.

The small population, consisting of some 753,000 people[1] living in poor and isolated agricultural villages, was an amalgam. As in ancient times, the modern Greeks had absorbed a number of their invaders and conquerors. In the words of Nikos Kazantzakis: "Just as the peoples of ancient Greece were a mixture of the most various races . . . so our contemporary peoples . . . have absorbed Slavs, Albanians, Franks, Arabs and Turks. . . . We cannot claim to be an aged and vulnerable race. We are young . . . our blood is still bubbling, unfermented."[2]

CENTRAL GREECE. For emotional reasons, if no other, the new nation had to be built around Athens. But there were other reasons. Attica, the province in which Athens is located, and the rest of the belt of small provinces stretching across the center of the country were important to the new Greece. The wooded mountains and water of the northeast part of these provinces were needed by a country long since denuded of most of its wood and sadly lacking in water. Most important was the Acheloos River, the longest in Greece, destined to be the seat of future hydroelectric developments, which by the mid-1960s has begun to revolutionize the Greek economy.

The central part of the country also possessed rich farmlands which were, and still are, of particular advantage because of their proximity to Athens. Forming a crude triangle between the sea and the mountains, Attica was a country of barren rocks and poor vegetation, but farmlands covered its central part, the Mesogeion. The farms produced the cereals and olives needed in the Athens trade, and their grapes were combined with resin from the pines of nearby Mount Penteli to make retsina, the pungent local wine. Another central province, Boeotia, also has long provided rich agricultural produce. Below the foothills of the mountains lies the large Boeotian plain, smiling and fruitful; in the midst of the plain is Thebes, where, according to mythology, Oedipus and Antigone lived, and which now is a medium-sized market town. In modern as in ancient Greece the Boeotian plain, like the Mesogeion, has always prospered when Athens has prospered.

ATHENS. Although Nauplia, Patras, and Corinth had at least equal commercial advantages with Athens so that Nauplia was chosen as the first capital of the new Greece in 1827, the historic claims of Athens were so great that six years later it became the capital. But Athens had been bitterly ravaged by invasions, occupations, neglect, and time. What had been left at the beginning of the nineteenth century of the low houses fronting many of the narrow, crooked streets had been burned down during the fight for independence so that only a few of the houses clustered on the northern and eastern slopes of the Acropolis remained when the capital was transferred there. Fortunately the fighting of the war for independence had done little damage to the Parthenon; it remained as it had been when the irreparable catastrophe of 1687 had struck it. In that year, the Parthenon, used as an Ottoman powder magazine, had its center blown out under the impact of a shell shot during the Venetian bombardment of the city. The Athens of today is largely new, rebuilt by Bavarian architects under the nation's first king, who stamped the city with an early nineteenth century west European look.

The city was destined to become a magnet in modern as it had been in ancient Greece, the capital and center of the nation's culture as well as of its trade, industry, and shipping. When independence came to Greece the city was so run down that no one could have foreseen the rise in population between 1951 and 1961 from 1,378,000 to 1,852,000 or by more than a third, while the rest of the country had increased by not quite a tenth, from 7,630,000 to 8,380,000. In 1958 Athens had some 47 per cent of all the industrial establishments of the country and 53 per cent of all employment in manufacturing; only five years later the city alone accounted for 65 per cent of the increase in the total number of establishments, and 85 per cent of the growth of all industrial employment. And the city continued to grow.

THE PELOPONNESE. Across the Gulf of Corinth and the Gulf of Patras from the northern mainland is the peninsula of the Peloponnese, which has always played an important role in Greek political history. Near its northern coast, where the mountains of Achaia rise stony and precipitous above the water, the ancient cities of Mycenae and Thebes were leaders in early civilization, with a high degree of artistic culture but with tragedy for the kings and queens of the house of Atreus. During the Byzantine Empire and the Frankish and Venetian occupations, much of the Peloponnese became prosperous. But soon after the midfifteenth century, when the Ottomans had captured most of the area, its rich farmlands were left idle.

THE KYKLÁDES. Of all the islands in the seas surrounding Greece, only Euboea, so close to the Attic mainland as to be almost a part of it, and the Kykládes in the central Aegean were part of the nation of Greece when it was formed.

Clustering like a chaplet around the rocky island of Delos, the great shrine of Apollo in the ancient world, the starkly beautiful but barren Kykládes were among those islands ceded to Venice in the partition of the Byzantine Empire in 1204. Subsequently owned by one great Venetian family after another, the islands held out against the Ottomans for over three hundred years. So strong was the influence of Venice and the Roman Catholic Church that the Kykládes, like the Ionians, in language and religion still show the marks of their long years under Venetian control.

The Kykládes are so poor that the inhabitants have found it difficult to scratch a living from the barren soil or the overfished seas around them. Combined with their exposed location which laid them open to constant harassment by pirates, the poverty of the islands has led to continued emigration of a number of their inhabitants.

Soon after the mideighteenth century, Russia decided to encourage anti-Ottoman sentiment in Greece and in the Russo-Turkish War (1768–1774) landed troops and secret agents in the Peloponnese. The Russians were, however, unsuccessful, and their fleet sailed away and occupied a number of the Kykládes. Their occupation of these islands, however, gradually dwindled away. No one strongly objected to the inclusion of the islands within the new Greece. It was not dreamed that the depopulated and poverty-stricken Kykládes, especially Mykonos and Naxos, would later achieve a considerable measure of prosperity from artists and tourists who would come to delight in their sun, their sculptured beauty, and the vivid contrasts of the seas around them.

The "Great Idea"

From the beginning the Greeks realized that the years of insurrection had brought them an incomplete nation. When the nation was formed in 1827 and 1832, the interests of the protecting powers, the continuing Ottoman control in a number of areas with large Greek populations, and the bitter divisions and rivalries within the infant state combined to prevent the inclusion within it of many people who were Greek in background. More people who were Greek in all but the accident of birthplace were excluded than included. In the Balkans and at the eastern end of the Mediterranean were large concentrations of people whose roots were Greek, whose language was Greek, who were of the Greek Orthodox faith, and who had a profound attachment to the Greek past.

Few if any of them would have been excluded from Herodotus' definition of Greek brotherhood as it had existed in the ancient world: "our common ancestry and language, the altars and sacrifices of which we all partake, and the common characteristics which we all bear." Like the Greeks living within the confines of the new Greece, these people on the outside were woven in a seamless web with the Greek past and with all other Greeks. Thus they formed part of the appeal of the new nation for enlargement of territory.

Long before the formation of modern Greece, there had been a dream that all Greeks should be united in one nation, as they had been in the Byzantine Empire. Witness to the dream may still be seen on the walls of the Historical Museum of Iraklion in Crete, where there is a "Dream Map of Great Greece," published in Venice in 1797. The map shows both Asia Minor and what is now Bulgaria within the confines of Greece.

With the birth of the Greek nation and the inevitable nationalism accompanying it, the idea grew steadily in Greek thought that all territory outside of Greece where there were substantial numbers of Greeks or those of Greek descent was *terra irredenta.* For over a hundred years annexation of those lands and their incorporation into the Greek nation became the great national goal, the impelling daemon, and the basis of the foreign and domestic policies of the new Greece. The drive, to which everything else in national policy became secondary, was a profoundly unifying force for the Greeks but a disruptive force for those of their neighbors whose borders contained large Greek minorities.

So widespread was the desire for extension of the nation's frontiers to include all Greeks and those of Greek ancestry that the earliest important candidate for the throne of Greece, Prince Leopold of Saxe-Coburg, a strong philhellene, made extension of territory beyond that provided by protocol of 1830 a condition of his acceptance of the throne. After taking it, he changed his mind and refused, in considerable part because of his disapproval of the frontier lines. Othon I, who accepted the throne and became the first king of Greece in 1832, had a romantic and passionate belief in the same cause. The nation as constituted that year was already somewhat larger than the one offered to Leopold in that it included the provinces of Acarnania and Aetolia.

It was chiefly the statesman Eleutherios Venizelos, born in Crete in 1863 and nurtured in the burning Cretan ambition for union (*énosis*) with Greece, who carried the torch of what came to be called the "Great Idea" or "Grand Ideal" (*Megali Idea*), the consolidation of the Greek people as they had been territorially and culturally under the Byzantine Empire.

From 1832 onward, the pieces in the Greek territorial jigsaw puzzle began to fall into place. Gradually various lands were secured by Greece, and various peoples of Greek background were brought under its jurisdiction. With them came others, including Bulgarians and Turks. Up to the end of the first quarter of the twentieth century most of those of Greek background remaining outside Greece were in Turkish or Bulgarian territory.

It took war to settle the situation. When the Greeks were defeated by the Turks in 1922–1923 the Great Idea became less appealing to many Greeks and especially to Venizelos. Yet Greece was to have more people of Greek background come under its jurisdiction as a result of that defeat than it might have secured by victory and direct acquisition of territory.

With the end of World War II the bitterness between Greece and Turkey over Cyprus began to grow and served as a sharp reminder that the Great Idea was neither entirely achieved nor entirely dead. When the matter became a subject of United Nations concern, discussion centered on the problem of the Turkish minority in Cyprus. But the Greeks never forgot that the island's population was approximately 80 per cent Greek in background.

Additions to Greek Territory

Despite the strength of the Great Idea in the nineteenth and twentieth centuries, the pieces in the Greek territorial picture were fitted together slowly and tortuously, as in a complicated picture puzzle. Some lands and peoples became part of Greece by negotiation and agreement, usually at the end of a war, but the largest number of Greeks from other lands reached Greece as the result of mass flight and population exchange in the early 1920s.

THE IONIAN ISLANDS, 1864. The first addition of territory and people of Greek background to the young nation came nearly forty years after the formation of the new Greece when England ceded the Ionian Islands to Greece. Formerly called Heptanesus because they number seven, the Ionians were desired by Greece for a number of reasons. Located between Italy and the coast of the Greek mainland, the islands had already formed a bridge for two-way commerce between East and West.

Although the people of the Ionians were chiefly Greek in background, the location of the islands made them continuously subject to Italian as well as Greek influences. During the four centuries in which various Venetian nobles dominated the islands, they fostered a certain amount of aristocratic spirit and developed an Italianate upper class; but they also laid the foundations for some self government. The Ionian people nevertheless remained essentially Greek, keeping for the most part their own Orthodox religion and Greek language, but mixing the language with some Italian words and pronunciation.

The Ottoman Empire, capturing and controlling the Ionians only briefly, never obtained a lasting foothold there. After the fall of Venice in 1797, the Ionians were tossed from Venetian to French, then to Russian control, and back to French, until they were captured by the English in 1809–1810. Some fifteen years later they were set up as an English protectorate, which they remained until growing Ionian commerce with Greece and steadily increasing insistence within the islands for union with the Greek mother country convinced England that the Ionians were of little value to it. England turned them over to Greece in 1864.

THESSALY, 1881. The next addition of lands and peoples came in 1881. The Greeks had never been content with the original northern boundary which cut them off not only from definitely Greek peoples but also from the rich plains of Thessaly, the small but productive plain of Arta, and the one

truly fertile section of Epirus. Worked out after long negotiation by the protecting powers, the boundary line of 1881 gave
Greece almost all of Thessaly and ran eastward from the
Thessalian coast to the point at which the Pinios (Peneus)
River enters the Aegean through the green gorge of the
ancient Vale of Tempe. Ending at the Ambracian Gulf of the
Ionian Sea on the west, the frontier now included within
it the town and district of Arta but not the rest of the province
of Epirus.

By the acquisition of Thessaly, Greece secured an area with
traditions deep in the Greek past. Even during the long Ottoman occupation of the area, Greeks had formed the majority
of the Thessalian population, and Greek had been the official
language. Important for the economic future of the whole
country was the richness and vastness of the area. Towered
over by almost 10,000 foot-high Mount Olympus, the vast
Thessalian plain was destined to contribute notably to the
Greek economy of the future by its large production of tobacco and grain. Nearby the slopes of Mount Pelion next
to its twin, Mount Ossa, were destined to provide some of
the wood much needed by the country. The capital, Larisa,
had long been a crossroads for communication between northern and central Greece and was to be an even more important
junction in the future.

CRETE, 1913. Old in its aspiration to join the Greek nation
but failing to achieve its wish until the end of a long and
bitter war was the beautiful and turbulent island of Crete.
Cretan uprisings had become frequent during the four centuries of Venetian occupation; in the almost two hundred
and thirty years of Ottoman control the Cretans rose again
and again against the occupying authorities.

The Cretans had an unflagging zeal for freedom and union

with Greece. But the island had to wait many years more for that union. The protecting powers apparently regarded Crete as too remote and too rich a prize to be given to the new nation at the dawn of its independence. Crete, furthermore, had a large Ottoman minority.

Uprisings against occupying Ottomans and Egyptians continued, and the protecting powers finally arranged the departure of the last Ottoman soldiers in November 1898. Although recognizing the continued sovereignty of the Sultan, the powers allowed Crete to form a constitution for an autonomous government, under the four-power control of England, France, Russia, and Greece, with Crown Prince George of Greece high commissioner.

After nearly seven hundred years of occupation by Venetians and Ottomans, the Cretans were jubilant. They believed union with Greece was at hand. The atmosphere is vividly portrayed by Nikos Kazantzakis, himself a witness: "On December 8, 1898, the day when Crete's betrothed, the Prince of Greece, set foot on Cretan soil, the whole of my inner heart was adorned, like all Greece that day, with myrtles and laurels."[3] But the myrtles and laurels faded; autonomy was not what the Cretans wanted, and long years lay ahead before Crete was finally incorporated in Greece in 1913.

MACEDONIA AND EPIRUS, 1913; THE EASTERN AEGEAN ISLANDS, 1914. The Great Idea came nearer to fulfillment at the end of the Balkan Wars, which brought Greece the vast areas of the northernmost province of Macedonia, the remaining parts of Epirus not yet given to Greece, and most of the islands of the eastern Aegean except the Dodecanese. Increasing in size from 25,000 to just under 42,000 square miles, in population from 2,666,000 to 4,363,000,[4] Greece also attained a long-wished-for sense of accomplishment. The eastern frontier of Greece extended to the mouth of the Mesta (Nestos) River on the Aegean. With increased size and longer borders came new military and border-control problems.

From earliest times, the Macedonian area of the Balkans had been a crossroad of migrating peoples and a pathway for invasions and trade. Gradually this mountainous area had become filled with mixed peoples—Greeks, Bulgars, Serbs, Vlachs, Turks, Jews, and still others—who together were to form the nucleus of the "Macedonian problem" of later times. In the early Middle Ages the independent kingdoms of the Serbs and Bulgars had each ruled the area, and throughout the late nineteenth and early twentieth centuries Serbia and Bulgaria again tried to secure it. The Greeks, on the other hand, had a long historical claim to Greek Macedonia, going back at least as far as Philip II. After the fall of Constantinople, Macedonia had remained a bulwark of Byzantine culture and of the Greek language and religion.

In the early nineteenth century the chaos of conflicting national interests in Macedonia became so great that it was placed under international control for nine years, beginning in 1905. But that control was not entirely successful. Meanwhile, the Young Turks rising in Thessaloniki in 1909 not only deposed the Sultan but also brought Greece's interests clearly into the open. Insisting that the Greek government disclaim any interest in the constant disturbances in Macedonia, Epirus, and especially Crete, the Young Turks were instrumental in causing the revolt in Athens of the Military League. The League's officers were dissatisfied with the way the Cretan situation in particular was being handled, as will be seen in Chapter 4, but they also desired to annex Macedonia.

After Greece joined in the Balkan Wars in the autumn

of 1912, the army of the Greek crown prince—soon to become King Constantine I—pushed their way through southwest Macedonia and entered the city of Thessaloniki amid great jubilation. During the second Balkan War Greece captured all of Macedonia, and the peace treaty of August 1913 gave to Greece a large part of the area, including the city of Kavalla, destined to become one of the most important tobacco exporting ports of Greece.

Although Greece had been given the town and district of Arta in western Epirus in 1881, it was not until the end of the Balkan Wars in 1913 that the southern and central parts of the province, including its capital Ioannina, came into Greek hands. The northern section, called *Northern Epirus* by the Greeks and *Southern Albania* by the Albanians, had been made part of Albania when it had been set up as a separate nation in 1912, and remains a part in the late 1960s. The dispute over this northern area is the reason for the technical state of war still existing between Greece and Albania.

The province held much appeal for the Greeks. It had been a last stronghold of the Byzantine Empire, and a majority of the people were Greek and had staunchly maintained their Greek traditions during the more than four hundred and fifty years of Ottoman control. Apart from the richness of the plain of Arta and the trading advantages of the location of Ioannina, much of the province of Epirus was an economic liability to Greece. As a whole that section is so ruggedly mountainous that the land has not been able to provide a decent living for the people and is altogether so poor that in recent years more emigrants have left it than any other province in Greece.

On its western coast the Epirot Mountains rise sheer and straight from the water, although two tiny ports provide a small western gateway from the sea to northern Greece.

The interior of the province is interlaced with small streams which become raging torrents in winter and carry the ravages of already existing erosion steadily further. The valleys of Epirus are completely secluded. Even in the late 1960s the province has no railways, and donkeys still are the principal means of transportation to the outside world.

Although Italy occupied the southeastern Aegean islands, Rhodes, and the other Dodecanese in 1912, the islands of the northeastern Aegean were so close to the Turkish coast that their disposition at the end of the Balkan Wars was a difficult matter. Many of the islands had been occupied by the Greeks during the Second Balkan War, but the peace treaty between Greece and Turkey of November 1913 failed to settle their future. Most of them, except Tenedos and Imbros, which guard the entrance to the Dardanelles, were turned over to Greece early in 1914.

THRACE, 1919. Like eastern Macedonia adjoining it, Thrace contained a mixture of peoples at least as early as the sixth to seventh centuries of the Christian era, when the Slavs had swept down and flooded the land with settlers.

Thrace's far eastern location brought it early under Ottoman control. It remained particularly subject to their influence. After capturing the area in the midfourteenth century, the Ottomans held it for over five hundred years before it was turned over to newly created Bulgaria in 1878, after the Russo-Turkish War. The Bulgarians controlled Thrace until 1919, when, as a result of the defeat of the Central Powers at the close of World War I, Bulgaria was required to cede the western part of the area to Greece. In that same year a first exchange of populations was provided. Greeks residing in Bulgaria who wanted to return to Greece were exchanged for an equal number of Bulgarians wishing to leave their residence in western Thrace for Bulgaria. The arrangements, as will be seen, took much time to carry out.

Balkan borders have always been subject to dispute, and those of Thrace have been no exception. Thrace in Greece is a geographic continuation of Thrace in Turkey, and the two are divided by the Maritsa River, also called the Hebrus, which drains the area and enters the Aegean near Samothrace. In 1919 the boundary of Thrace between Greece and Turkey was established at the Maritsa as it once had been. By the late 1960s the river has become one of the hopeful signs in Greco-Turkish relations because it is the site of a great modern dam under construction which it is expected will provide irrigation for the surrounding areas of both countries.

THE DODECANESE, 1948. The last important additions of territory to Greece came at the end of World War II with the cession by a defeated Italy of the Dodecanese Islands (which number thirteen and not twelve as their name indicates). Like the large islands of the north Aegean, the Dodecanese always had great strategic and trading importance because of their accessibility in the Mediterranean and their closeness to the coast of Anatolian Turkey. The large island of Rhodes is only eleven miles from the Turkish coast.

Chiefly Greek in population, the Dodecanese had been taken by the Italians from the Turks during the Italo-Turkish War in 1912. The islands continued to be held by Italy despite the expressed desire of an island congress for union with Greece. When the end of World War II forced Italy to give up all its colonial possessions, the Dodecanese, including Rhodes, was made part of Greece, although not until 1948 were the formalities of cession completed.

With this addition of territory, the nation attained the size and area which, save for minor border adjustments, have con-

Growth of Modern Greece, 1821–1948. (Adapted from W. W. Heurtley, H. C. Darby, C. W. Crawley, and C. M. Woodhouse, *A Short History of Modern Greece,* page 101 [Cambridge: at the University Press].)

tinued in the late 1960s. By piecemeal additions the country has about doubled its original size, and many thousands of people of Greek background or extraction, and of language, religion, and national feeling, have been added to the population. Save for their unabated desire for the *énosis* of Cyprus and "Northern Epirus" with Greece, the Greeks had attained

most of the aims of the Great Idea soon after World War
II and so would have been ready to turn their energies to the
internal development of their country and the peaceful
growth of their international relations if other tragedies had
not intervened.

*Increase in the Greek People by Exchange of Populations in
the 1920s*

The largest increase in the Hellenic population of Greece
came as the result of war and horror. Long before the Ottoman occupation of Greece, many Turks and other Ottoman
peoples had moved into Greece. Some had come of their own
volition, and many more had been taken to Greece from the
eighth to the fourteenth centuries by the Byzantine emperors
who needed their services to fight the Bulgars and Serbs.
Many of the Ottoman recruits remained in Greece. But it
was in modern times, through the cession of Thessaly, parts
of Macedonia, and of western Thrace to Greece that brought
under the Greek flag the large numbers of Turks living in
those areas.

At the end of World War I, the Treaty of Sèvres was
proposed to conclude peace between the Allies and the Ottoman Empire. It was signed but never ratified. Among its
provisions was one that the city of Smyrna, inhabited largely
by Greeks, together with its hinterland, be turned over to
Greece, for administration for a period of five years. While
the treaty remained unratified the Turks, in a wave of mount-
ing nationalism, began to harass the Greek residents of the
Smyrna area and elsewhere along the Anatolian coast. Prime
Minister Venizelos proposed, and Britain and France approved, a Greek offensive against the Turks to compel them
to accept the terms of the unapproved treaty providing for
Greek administration of the area.

Believing they had Allied backing, the Greeks landed their forces on the western coast of Anatolia on April 13, 1919. The war-weary Allies, divided in their ideas for settlement and especially over policies toward revolutionary Russia, failed to back up the expedition. The Greeks, fighting alone, were unable to weather the storm. Under the leadership of Mustafa Kemal Pasha, the famous Ataturk (who had been born in Thessaloniki of a Turkish family), the Turks pushed the Greek armies before them to the coast. Tens of thousands of refugee Greeks fled at the same time, and others from the north of Turkey took refuge in the northeastern provinces of Greece. In the autumn of 1922 the city of Smyrna was sacked and burned to the ground and only a remnant of the Greeks living there managed to escape.

After the disaster it appeared that the only way to settle the problem of the homeless and fleeing civilian Greeks in Turkey was a massive population exchange. As provided by the Treaty of Lausanne in 1923, nearly 1,500,000 Greeks left Turkey for Greece and some 400,000 Turks left Greece for Turkey. Soon thereafter, about 40,000 Greeks and 40,000 Bulgarians were exchanged between Greece and Bulgaria, according to proposed terms of the Treaty of Sèvres hitherto not carried out.

For the most part, the new arivals were settled around Athens, in Crete, and especially in northern Greece. The authors well remember their first visit to Athens in 1929, when huts and tents as far as the eye could reach sheltered many thousands of refugees. Then, and for some time thereafter, the problem of assimilation of such vast numbers of people appeared well-nigh insoluble, but the refugees—progressive and industrious—in the long run became a great asset to Grece.

A small number of Greeks in Turkey and of Turks in Greece were not part of the population exchange. Some

80,000 Greeks were allowed to remain in Istanbul, and perhaps 100,000 Turkish Muslims stayed in western Thrace at
the time. Later other Turks crossed the border from Turkey
and remained in Greece. In the Dodecanese, some 8,000
Turks stayed on. For the most part living in separate villages,
the Turkish population within Greece continued to lead their
separate lives because of differences from the Greeks in religion and custom.

Even after the Cyprus crisis became acute in December
1963, when relations between Greece and Turkey were at a
low ebb, a number of people of Turkish ethnic origin nevertheless remained in Greece; for instance, in villages on the
island of Rhodes the Turkish minority kept to their daily
routine, apparently undisturbed by events outside the country.
In some places they were not equally contented, as for instance in Thrace. In the late 1960s Turkey complained that
all was not well with the Turkish minority resident there.
Some people believed this was an attempt to stir up political
trouble because of other tensions between Greece and Turkey.

Increasing Hellenization of the Greek Population

After Greece became an independent nation in 1827 new-
comers to the population were predominantly of Greek
background, language, and religion. The additions of new
territories brought chiefly Greeks (in the same sense) under
the flag of the new nation. The greatest Hellenization of the
population, however, came with the vast numbers of people
of ethnic Greek background who poured into the country
as refugees or parts of the population exchanges. The same
exchanges removed the majority of the Turks and Bulgarians
and thus produced a more homogeneous population.

The smaller numbers of refugees who later fled to Greece

were also of Hellenic background. After Nasser took power in Egypt approximately 80,000 Greeks, most of them prosperous merchants, middle-class tradesmen, or technicians, were forced out of Egypt and moved to Greece. There their abilities and skills proved more important than their numbers. In 1930 more than 100,000 people of Greek background or nationality lived in Istanbul; most of them had been born and had always lived in Turkey. In the heat of the Cyprus crisis of 1964 and 1965 a number of Greek nationals were expelled and others fled to Greece so that altogether some 60,000 arrived in Greece. Many felt spiritually at home, but others were so completely uprooted by the change that by 1967 they had not yet become adjusted to it.

Differences among the Greeks

The Greeks vary widely among themselves. The mountain barriers, the separation of the islands, and the lack of easy communication between different parts of the country combined to bring out striking differences between the people of one section and another. Those whose ancestors had lived on the Anatolian coast for centuries, reaching Greece in the exchange of populations, differed widely in outlook from those whose forebears had lived on the Greek mainland or on the islands. A number of observers believed that the uprooting made the new arrivals more adaptable than those long undisturbed in their homes and ways of life.

Each Greek has great pride in the section of the country from which he comes and to a certain extent looks down on those from other places. "To the world at large a man may be a Greek but to other Greeks he is a Macedonian, an Arcadian or an Epirot. More than this, he comes from a particular village of which he is very proud."[5] There are often differences between the people of one village and those of a neighboring one, and among people of the same island. On Crete, albeit a large island, the villagers of the low and sloping shores of the east coast are reported to be more outgoing than the somewhat dour peasants of the harsh and isolated western mountains. The differences appear even in their handicrafts; the colors of the embroideries done by the women of the east coast are softer than the reds and blacks of the west.

Greece's Absorption of Minorities

Except in the northern provinces Greece's politics have been little complicated by recalcitrant and unassimilated minority groups. Centuries ago the Greeks not only had conquered almost all their invaders culturally but also had assimilated many of them in language, religion, and even custom. As time passed, few minority groups in Greece remained outside the essential pattern of its life. By the 1960s all the minorities together constituted less than 4 per cent of the population, but this small percentage for the most part has kept their languages and ways.

THE VLACHS. A separate group who have been in Greece at least since the Middle Ages but have managed to keep their own customs and their own language while often becoming involved in politics are the Vlachs (Koutsovlachs). They are non-Greek in origin and are believed to be the descendants of Roman colonists and Latinized provincials from both sides of the Danube. The Vlachs originally called themselves Romans, but their neighbors near the Danube referred to all Roman provincials as Vlachs, a Slavonic term meaning *strangers*. From the earliest times the Vlachs have been shepherds and nomadic herdsmen, wandering through the Balkans and the north of Greece. On their early migrations they gave the Vlach name to various districts, including the province of Wallachia in present-day Romania and Little Wallachia or Acarnania in Greece.

By the late twelfth century the Vlachs had already become involved in a revolt against the Byzantine Empire. They appeared again in history among those trying to stem the Ottoman advance at the battle of Kossevo in 1389. The Vlachs had been in Greece so many generations by the time of the Greek War of Independence that they took part in the struggle and contributed several leaders to the cause. Those Vlachs living in the Ottoman Empire were given particular privileges by the Sultan in 1905 and then were used in an attempt to stir up trouble between the Greeks and Romanians, to whom the Vlachs have a vague kinship and whose language resembles theirs. In still later years various groups tried to play on the different background of the Vlachs from that of other Greeks. The Germans during World War II and the Communists in countries north of Greece during the years of guerrilla fighting made attempts, for the most part unsuccessful, to win the Vlachs away from Greek allegiance. In the 1960s the Vlachs for the most part were Greek in national consciousness and feelings, if not in language.

Continuing in Greece as a group apart, the Vlachs are Greek Orthodox in religion, but still speak Greek only as a second language, and with an accent akin to Romanian. In the late 1960s, they live as they always have, as wide-ranging shepherds, leading their flocks down from the deep snows and chill rains of the mountains in late autumn and returning for the high, cool greenness and vegetation of summer. The Vlachs also have permanent village homes, such as Metsova, high on the east-west road across the Pindus

Mountains. In this picturesque village in the mid-1960s the authors have watched the Vlachs on a Sunday morning, when the women's church costumes of vivid reds and blues contrasted strikingly with the green of the spring fields and the clear blue of the sky.

THE SARAKATSÁNS. Frequently confused with the Vlachs is another group of nomadic shepherds, the Sarakatsáns, who have played a part in modern Greek history. Although their exact origins are unknown, the Sarakatsáns are believed by a number of students to be the oldest and possibly the purest Greeks. For countless generations they have married only among themselves, and in their remote mountains have been little diluted by the waves of invasion which have swept through Greece from time immemorial. The Sarakatsáns have always spoken Greek, and "no one challenges the Greekness of the Sarakatsáns; all of them share common origins, customs, languages, and a way of life."[6] They have developed few fixed abodes and, as shepherds and herdsmen from the dark ages, they antedated the Vlachs in wandering the remote and rugged mountains. Like the Cretan and Maniot mountaineers during the centuries of Ottoman occupation, they were able to escape the tax collectors, and "they say, perhaps a shade boastfully: 'we and the monasteries were the backbone of all the revolutions against the Turks.' "[7]

THE JEWS. Beginning in the twelfth century, a number of dispersed Jews established communities in the cities of Greece, where they founded proud and vital groups which did much for the commercial and civic life of the cities but took comparatively little part in the politics. In the Middle Ages, two thousand or more Jews lived in Thebes and were reported to be "the most skilled artificers in silk and purple cloth throughout Greece."[8] Later, when thousands of Jews were expelled from Spain under Ferdinand and Isabella, the Ottomans offered these Jews asylum. Many settled in Thessaloniki and remained there. In the sixteenth century the Jewish community was organized into an autonomous state which associated itself with the commercial interests of Venice. With the decline of Venice and the quarrels which split the Jews into bitter factions, the Jewish community had passed the zenith of its power by the end of the seventeenth century.

Throughout the centuries, the number of Jews increased, especially in Thessaloniki and Athens. Before World War II, Thessaloniki, with 60,000 to 70,000 Jewish inhabitants, ranging from day laborers to rich merchants, was one of the largest Jewish centers in the eastern Mediterranean. Almost completely autonomous, they spoke their own language and lived in a community considerably apart from the rest of the people of the city. At the end of World War II the Jewish numbers had been reduced to less than two thousand. By the mid-1960s, more than five thousand are living in Thessaloniki again, and with new industrial and commercial developments the city is proving a loadstone for others to take up life and work there.

THE ALBANIANS. Appearing in Greece somewhat later than the Vlachs, the Albanians have played a long and important political part in modern Greek history. Beginning approximately in the fourteenth century, many Albanians were taken to Greece as workers for the great landlords, and later others left their homes in the mountainous north, in or near what is now Albania, and poured into Greece in waves. Many went as mercenaries for the Byzantine rulers of the Peloponnese in their struggle to hold off the advancing Ottomans. Then came Albanian colonists who settled on desolate lands in the

Peloponnese, in Attica (including especially the island of Euboea), and in Boeotia. In both Euboea and Boeotia the Albanians were first put to work to restore land which had been laid waste by marauding Catalan mercenaries. The Florentines, in strong control of Epirus in the fifteenth and sixteenth centuries, imported Albanian workers from the area immediately north of Epirus. The Venetians, occupying Boeotia and some of the smaller islands, also found the use of Albanian laborers important to complete their work.

Although a number of the early Albanian settlers were taken into Greece to help ward off the attacks of the Ottomans, some Albanians later began to work for them. In the seventeenth century, possibly acting under Venetian pressure, the Albanians of the Peloponnese rose against their Ottoman employers in a far-reaching revolt which devastated the surrounding countryside. But within the next one hundred years the Albanians for the most part became imbued with the love of Greece, and in the War for Independence provided some of the country's foremost national leaders. For all the Greek outlook of the Albanians settled in Greece, however, they still retained a considerable separate identity. Even in the late 1960s they live in their own colonies in many of the areas where they had been settled centuries ago, and continue to speak their own Albanian dialect.

"SLAVOPHONES." Chief among the minorities who continue as distinct groups in the late 1960s are the "Slavophones," who still speak a Slavic language. They remained in Macedonia and Thrace after the population exchange of the early 1920s. Many were Slav Macedonians who preferred to stay on their own lands rather than emigrate but who continued to retain a consciousness of their relationship to Bulgaria. Many others among the number who stayed were Slav-speaking Greeks. At that time Greece officially classified them all as Greeks speaking a Slavic language and was unwilling to have them included under the minority treaties of the League of Nations.

The northern Slavs were destined "to form a complicating factor in the 'Macedonian problem' of future times"[9] in relation to the other Balkan nations and particularly when those countries became Communist at the end of World War II. Unlike the Slavs of southern Greece who had absorbed the life and language of the country, the Slavic groups of the northern Greek provinces have always spoken a Slavic language intermingled with Greek words; and they have followed the Bulgarian rite of the Orthodox Church since it became separate in 1876 with the establishment of the modern Bulgarian nation.

Probably fewer than 50,000 "Slavophones" remain in Greece in the late 1960s.[10] Twenty to thirty years ago, a number had been seduced from Greece by Communist propaganda for a separate Macedonian state. During the guerrilla fighting of the years before 1949 many of these people of Slavic consciousness and Communist inclination had fled to Yugoslavia and the other countries north of the border. When the Yugoslav borders were closed in 1949 and when the Communists were defeated in Greece the same year many more fled to Albania and Bulgaria, while still others were abducted. In 1950 both Greek and Yugoslav sources indicated that over 50,000 "Macedonian" refugees were living in Yugoslavia alone.[11] During subsequent decades most of the Communist refugees remained in those coutries, many because they were unable to obtain permission to return to Greece. A few were cleared sufficiently to be allowed to go back, and a thin trickle slipped clandestinely across the borders.

Appendix to Chapter 3—Cyprus Not Part of Modern Greece

Over 9,000 square miles in size, Cyprus is the third largest island in the Mediterranean, after Sicily and Sardinia. Located halfway between Turkey and Syria in the southeastern Mediterranean, the island has always been prized for its location and its wealth, notably in copper. (The word copper is derived from the name Cyprus.) In late Achaean times waves of Greek settlers moved to Cyprus, and in approximately the same era Phoenician seafarers from Asia Minor also settled on the island. Thus early in its history Cyprus was already a meeting place of two cultures. In the mid-1950s, between 80 and 82 per cent of its 600,000 inhabitants were of Greek extraction; the remainder were of Turkish ancestry and language, and of the Muslim religion.

Throughout the Christian era, Cyprus has always been a pawn on the Mediterranean chessboard. With the successful revolt of its ruler in the midtwelfth century, the disintegration of its relations with the Byzantine Empire began. After a brief period of independence, Cyprus was again taken by the Byzantine Empire; it later fell to the Arabs, to the Crusaders of Richard Coeur de Lion, the Knights Templar, the titular king of Jerusalem, the Genoese, the Venetians, and the Ottomans. The Ottomans conquered it in 1571 and remained the sole occupying power until the British took over administrative control in 1878, although leaving the island as part of the Ottoman Empire. When World War I broke out Britain annexed Cyprus and then, together with other Allied powers, offered to cede it to Greece in return for Greek aid to Serbia in the struggle against Germany; but the offer was not accepted. Greece, Britain, and Turkey were all nations "whose interest in Aphrodite's Isle could be termed less than vibrant."

In 1925, in the face of growing opposition to its continued presence in the island, Britain made it a crown colony, with parliamentary institutions. During World War II and then the Suez Crisis of 1956, Cyprus served Britain as an airbase and refueling station. However, as nationalism mounted, rioting and bloodshed grew.

Agreements were made in London and Zürich, and a constitution setting up the Republic of Cyprus was completed in 1959.

CHAPTER 4

Monarchy, Republics, and

Dictatorships before World War II

Desire by the Greeks for a government of their own choosing
was strengthened by their centuries under foreign domination; by the intellectual revival within the country in the
late eighteenth century; and by the ideas of liberty, fraternity,
and equality spread abroad by the French Revolution. Attempts during the years of insurrection to frame a constitution for the new nation nevertheless proved premature and
showed Greek interest in self-government but lack of modern experience in anything but rudimentary local government.

When independence came, emergent Greece was united
only in its desire for freedom and had little preconception of
the form of government which it might wish for its own.
Not until 1827, just before freedom was attained, was an
assembly, meeting in Troizin (Troezene), sufficiently representative of a considerable part of the country and unified
enough in purpose to draw up a constitution which launched
the new nation.

As foreign help had been required to complete Greek
liberation, the infant nation was tied to the leading strings
of England, France, and Russia. All three wanted to dominate
the new nation; each had its own interests and ambitions in
both Greece and Turkey, and especially in the Turkish straits

leading to Constantinople. Russia, which played an important part in the politics of emerging Greece, actively opposed the idea of a constitution for the new nation; England and France were entirely willing for Greece to have its own constitutional document but they did little to forward its development.

During the years of uprising, various intellectuals, educated in the West and under the particular influence of the ideology of the French Revolution, believed that their nation should be established as a republic, a fitting step in a land which had laid the foundations of the democratic idea more than two millenia earlier. Within the Greece of 1827, lines had not yet been clearly drawn between ardent believers in a republic and strong advocates of a monarchy. It remained for a later period to reveal the sharp differences between those who regarded a monarchy as a safeguard and those who believed it a menace to the tranquility of the country.

The three protecting powers agreed to the formation of the infant state as a republic, but with the understanding that it was to be temporary. All three were monarchies at the time, and all believed that their protegé should have the same form of government. Even before the republic was under way, the protecting powers had begun the search for a king of Greece. After agreeing with difficulty not to choose from their own reigning families, the powers looked into the availability of Prince Leopold of Saxe-Coburg as early as 1825, but he was not approached until five years later. He first accepted, then declined the throne, reportedly saying: "Whoever becomes king of Greece had better keep his bag packed"—a prediction destined to prove correct in more than one instance. Meanwhile, the republic set up by the Convention of Troizin lived with the constant reminder by the protecting powers that they were searching for a king to head the Greek nation.

The First Republic of Modern Greece and Its President,
Ioannis Capodistrias, 1827-1831

During the last days of the insurrection, just before the
protecting powers undertook the task of mediation between
the Greeks and the Ottomans, Ioannis Capodistrias was made
president of the infant republic. Born a member of the
prosperous and educated class in the Ionian Islands when
they were still under Venetian control, Capodistrias spent
much of his adult life away from home.

He became an educated cosmopolitan, so deeply affected
by his life outside Greece that it left a permanent imprint on
his conduct of affairs of state. He studied at the University of
Padua in Italy, and there witnessed part of Napoleon's campaign, an event which profoundly impressed him. Later
Capodistrias served the Czarist government of Russia, first in
its brief administration of the Ionian Islands, then on mission
to Switzerland, and finally as the Czar's secretary of state for
foreign affairs. The years in Russian employ developed in
him a belief in strong leadership and a conviction that all
actions for the welfare of the people should be instituted
from above. Although he was devoted to the ideal of freedom
for Greece, and spent much time and energy during his stay
in Switzerland trying to attract adherents to its cause, he disliked the military chieftains and local Greek notables who
formed so much of the country's insurrectionary leadership.

Fearing the power of those chieftains and the rivalries
among them, the Greek founding fathers had established a
weak executive for the republic under its first constitution, the
Convention of Troizin. Capodistrias, with his belief that only
strong leadership could weld the divided regions into one
nation, had little faith in the government over which he

presided. He did not believe, furthermore, that the Convention, drawn up when parts of Greece were still under Ottoman control, was valid for the whole country. Those who had no voice in the formation of a document could not be expected to have it apply to them.

First Steps toward Dictatorship under President Capodistrias

The republic of Capodistrias had various inherent weaknesses. It suffered from problems inevitable for a new nation and from particular difficulties associated with a temporary form of government kept under close surveillance by foreign powers. The death knell of the republic was sounded within a year after Capodistrias took office when he suspended the operation of the Convention and set up his own form of emergency government, organized nonetheless in accordance with carefully considered legal principles. Under it, legislative and executive powers were in the hands of the president, assisted by an advisory council, and necessary affairs of state were carried on by a series of periodically issued mandates. The first stones on the road to dictatorship had been laid.

Regarded as too favorable to Russia because of his past services to the Czar, Capodistrias was eyed skeptically by both England and France. Indirectly, if not directly, their suspicions aided a rebellion of the chieftains of the Mani in the southern and remote Taygetus Mountains. He had snubbed or affronted those chieftains, some of whom were sincere patriots, although others feared merely loss of power through him. In October 1831, after serving only four of his seven-year term, Capodistrias was assassinated by the son and brother of an important but imprisoned Mani chief.

Before Capodistrias' death, the government had been beset

by financial and, especially, factional troubles. So great did the disunity become that the new nation reached a virtual state of anarchy, which became even worse after Capodistrias' assassination. His followers set up one government, and other factions established a rival. Eventually all authority broke down. Within Greece the stage was set for the adoption of the foreign-sponsored idea of a monarchy.

First King of Modern Greece, Othon, 1833–1862

In the face of the chaos, many Greeks had come to believe that a monarchy might prove the solution for their difficulties. Its creation, however, was brought about by the protecting powers. When the republic ended in calamity, the powers indicated that they "had contributed decisively to Greek independence . . . and they had 'not only the right but the obligation' " to intervene.[1] This they did by means of a treaty in 1832, which declared Greece independent of the Ottoman Empire but placed it under the guardianship of the three powers. They selected Prince Otto, the seventeen-year-old son of the King of Bavaria, for king of Greece without consultation with the Greeks.

Because of Otto's extreme youth a regency was appointed by his father which exercised the rights of sovereignty during Otto's minority. After coronation as Othon (the Greek form of his name), King of Greece, he became an ardent champion of the Greeks and their national hopes— the first member of Greece's two foreign dynasties to become strongly Greek in outlook and emotion. During his almost thirty-year reign, King Othon nevertheless remained a Roman Catholic and a good Bavarian as well as a romantic believer in the Greek destiny. He imported his own artisans and even a brewer from Bavaria, a certain Fuchs, whose name, transliterated into Greek as Fix, remains today the name of a large Greek brewing concern.

For all the influence of its Byzantine and Ottoman background of administration, Greece appeared under King Othon to have systems of government, administration, and even of education which had become largely creatures of Bavarian influence. To the ideas of centralized administrative control inherited chiefly from French ideas and practice, King Othon added those of his native Bavaria. As early as his reign, Greece became locked in a system of centralized administration which has persisted throughout its subsequent history and has always been a cause of slow-moving and creaking governmental machinery.

Bavarian troops, with equipment and wages paid from the Greek treasury, were added by the King to the scattered forces remaining in Greece after the end of the republic. At the same time, the troops were released who had been maintained in Greece by the protecting powers. Officials, nominated by and responsible to as well as removable by the King, took the place which had been occupied by the Greek clergy in administering Greek affairs under the Ottomans. For all practical purposes Greece had become "a proctectorate of Bavaria, with an existence guaranteed by the protecting powers." Foreign influences thus continued to play a predominant part in the life of the young nation. To the primarily French and English influences, German had been added and would continue important for many years to come.

Revolts against King Othon's Rule

King Othon ruled his individualistic Greek subjects as an absolute monarch and in the tradition of centralized control of his native Bavaria. He was doubtless sincere in using the only methods of government which he knew and in believing that he was helping forward the cause of Greece to which he was deeply and romantically attached.

Despite his espousal of the desires of the Greeks, King Othon became increasingly unpopular in the nation which had had no voice in choosing him. Eleven years after his coronation there was a sudden revolt. A group of insurrectionary leaders and disappointed politicians believed that they had been deprived of their just rewards when the nation was formed and had also come to resent the dictatorial methods of the King, especially his Bavarian administrators and troops. Joined by members of the Athenian garrison, they engineered a coup in September 1843. Although the military forces were not the prime instigators, they aided in securing the withdrawal of the Bavarian troops. They also helped bring about the convocation of a National Assembly in 1844 which adopted a constitution setting up a two-chambered legislative body.

For over nineteen years the new Parliament accomplished little in lessening the King's power. He controlled the upper house by nominating all its members for life; he vetoed any legislative acts he did not like; and he governed by executive decree. He used the right of appointment and dismissal of ministers so frequently and created so many posts outside the regular ministries as to build up a personal political machine. For the second time in the life of the young nation, some of the stones of dictatorship had been trod.

King Othon's continued use of constitutional arrangements merely to suit his own ends led to growing objection, and finally to another revolt. Based on a wider popular appeal than in 1843, a revolt in 1862 was ignited by university students and middle-class intellectuals, and the flames were fanned by the army.

In the same period, the King incurred the enmity of all three of the protecting powers. England was disturbed by his strong pro-Hellenic stand and consequent refusal to aid in strengthening the Ottoman Empire which England needed as a potential ally against Russia. In its turn, Russia, strongly Orthodox in religion, was influenced against King Othon because he remained a Roman Catholic. Both England and Russia opposed his honest and passionate belief in the cause of Hellenism, with its concomitant wish to expand the nation's frontiers. In France Napoleon III believed that King Othon fomented constant insurrections throughout the Balkan peninsula in the hope of extending Greek territory further.

Having incurred the hostility of all the protecting powers and of many Greeks themselves, King Othon was deposed after the 1862 revolt, and his Bavarian dynasty expelled. It was indeed ironic that his determination to try to fulfill the Greek people's expansionist ideals became the chief cause of his downfall.

Later generations have been kinder in their estimate of King Othon than were his contemporaries. In the thirty years of his reign, "population and shipping had alike been doubled, and foreign trade (no doubt at its lowest ebb in 1833) had been more than quadrupled, only to be more than doubled again in the next decade. Athens had grown from a village into a small city . . . without repudiating a special relation to the protecting powers, the king had done his best to make Greece more nearly independent in fact."[2]

Search for Another King

Prince Alfred, son of Queen Victoria of England, was strongly favored for the throne by the Greeks, who voted approval of his nomination in their National Assembly. But as yet they had not been given the right to decide on their own governmental path or to choose their own sovereign. England vetoed the choice because of agreement with the other protecting powers that no candidate should be chosen from among any of their reigning families, and because it feared its support of the Ottoman Empire would be jeopardized by so close a tie to Greece. In view of the English unwillingness to accept Prince Alfred as a candidate and the difficulties of finding anyone who appeared suitable to them as well as to the other protecting powers, the Greeks asked England for other suggestions to help them out of the dilemma.

Nineteen-year-old Prince William George, second son of the heir to the Danish throne of the house of Glücksborg, was agreed on by all the protecting powers as king, and Greece was declared a "monarchical, independent and constitutional state" by treaty of the protecting powers and Denmark in July 1863.[3] Although the initiative for finding a monarch was still in foreign hands, the treaty of 1863, unlike that negotiated in 1832 without consultation with the Greeks, took into account the wishes of the Greek Assembly, which had agreed to Prince William George's selection. By the constitution completed in 1864, Greece's constitutional parliamentary monarchy or royal republic was established.

The House of Glücksborg's First King of the Hellenes, George I, 1863–1913

Young Prince William George was crowned in 1863 before the new constitution had been drawn up. Accepting for himself and his heirs the constitutional requirement of 1844 to profess the Greek Orthodox faith, the new monarch was crowned King George I of the Hellenes, not King of Greece as his predecessor had been. The change was important. The title appealed to the Greeks because it served as a double reminder, of the Byzantine emperors who had been referred to as emperors of the Hellenes and of the Greeks living in areas not incorporated into Greek territory at the time of the new king's coronation.

Ever since King George I ascended the throne of the Hellenes, Greece has had a Glücksborg as king, with few interruptions. When he was crowned, King George was said to be "courteous, kindly and physically mature but intellectually young for his age."[4] He was given an unfortunate start by Count Sponneck, the adviser provided by his father. Although the Count was supposed to train him in the duties of a monarch, Sponneck constantly referred to King George as "le jeune homme" and treated him accordingly. Finally it became clear that the Count was interfering so seriously in Greek government and politics that he could not be allowed to remain. He was forced to leave the country ten years after "the young man" had become king.

Under the influence of his adviser in the early years of his reign, King George was inclined to reign as an absolute monarch, exercising his powers with little difference, in essence, from the actions of King Othon. "Undeterred by the fate of his predecessor, [he] attempted to govern through minority or extra-parliamentary ministries on behalf of which he made lavish use of the weapon of dissolution. The consequences of this ill-advised course were ministerial instability, scandalous governmental interference with elections, administrative paralysis and corruption, and an alarming increase of anti-dynastic sentiment."[5] But gradually under the impetus of the constitution of 1864, King George I learned the art of serving as a constitutional monarch.

Many years of King George's reign were occupied with serious problems on the international front. The long struggle of the people of Crete and their sympathizers in Athens to secure *énosis* with Greece filled the years from 1866 onwards. Following the annexation of Thessaloniki and part of Epirus, Greece was plagued for many years by domestic difficulties, notably financial, caused by the expense of mobilizing and equipping an army and policing its long new borders.

Revolt of the Military League, 1909–1911

The many decades in which no progress had been made toward the annexation of Crete were disturbing to Greece, as were various upheavals in Macedonia, at least part of which also desired annexation. Within Greece, the growing cities, and particularly their trading and professional groups, felt that much needed to be done to improve economic conditions. As popular discontent increased, the dynasty of the Glücksborgs, the parliamentary system, and the monarchy all came under attack.

As a result of these dissatisfactions, a group of young army and navy officers of the lowest commissioned ranks organized themselves in a Military League. They were not only personally ambitious but they were also disillusioned with the handling of Greece's problems. In 1909 the officers at the Athens garrison joined in leading a revolt. Among their demands was the removal of Crown Prince Constantine and other members of the royal family from the armed forces, where they were thought to be exercising both personal and dynastic influence. The League members also wanted many of their demands embodied in constitutional forms.

By summoning Eleutherios Venizelos from his home island of Crete to be their adviser, the Military League unwittingly gave him his first opportunity to come to the front of the national stage. Already prominent in Crete, he rose to main-land fame rapidly and became prime minister of Greece in 1910. By the following year he was able to convince the League's officers that they should limit their demands to a revision of the constitution and then dissolve their organiza-tion. As prime minister, he pushed their constitutional re-visions which formed the basis of a constitution in 1911. Venizelos hoped it would provide orderly channels for gov-ernmental change and so prevent the interference of the army in politics, a hope destined not to be fulfilled in the forsee-able future.

End of George I's Reign, 1913

A crisis between Greece and Turkey came in October 1912, when Greece entered the war against Turkey being waged by the Balkan nations. The conquering army of Crown Prince Constantine then swept through southern and western Mace-donia. With Macedonia conquered and Crete by now vir-tually part of Greece, it seemed that the course of the mon-archy had been steadied. By a tragic turn of fate, in March 1913 the King went to Thessaloniki to assert the demand of the Greeks for the annexation of Macedonia. Walking unat-tended in the city streets only a few days before the fiftieth anniversary of his accession to the throne, he was shot.

The brother-in-law of King Edward VII of England and uncle of Czar Nicholas of Russia, King George I strengthened Greece's national aspirations and served his country well throughout his long stewardship. After the early part of his reign, he lessened his resort "to the dismissal of an unde-feated ministry or to his right of forming an extra-parlia-mentary cabinet. . . . the King's prudent restraint prevented criticism of his dynasty from becoming serious. . . . Unfor-tunately the corruption of politics and the violent intervention of the army had not been eliminated."[6] Both were destined to continue far into the future.

King Constantine I, 1913–1922

Under Constantine I, the son and successor of King George I, German influences again dominated the Greek scene. He had been a victorious leader and popular hero in the Epirot and Macedonian campaigns of the Balkan Wars just before he ascended the throne in 1913. So popular was he that some people hailed him as Constantine XII, the inheritor of the Byzantine tradition of Constantine XI, who had lost his life in the siege of Constantinople by the Ottomans in 1453. But the reign of Constantine I was destined to be less happy than that of his father, George I, to suffer serious interruptions, and to end in catastrophe.

In a union which became a determining factor in the future of his country, Constantine married the sister of Kaiser Wilhelm II of Germany. Profoundly impressed by the sight of the German armed forces proudly displayed by his brother-in-law, King Constantine I regretted that he was unable to influence Greece to join the Central Powers in World War I. Failing that, he tried to maintain Greece's neutrality and to prevent its entry into the war on the side of the Allies. Eleutherios Venizelos, many times prime minister, was opposed to German war aims and impressed by Allied naval power, which he believed necessary to help protect his sea-surrounded country.

Emergence of the "Constitutional Question"

When Venizelos attempted to secure King Constantine I's consent to Greek participation in the Gallipoli campaign on the side of the Allies, he and Constantine disagreed so seriously that the King dismissed him from the premiership despite his large majority in Parliament. Elected to office again the same year, Venizelos persuaded the King to invite English and French armed forces to Greece to aid in the protection of Serbia to the north. It was not long before Allied troops landed in Thessaloniki. Soon, however, King Constantine's sympathy for Germany reasserted itself and he again forced Venizelos to resign as prime minister, over the same issue of foreign policy, and for the second time in the same year. The stage was set and the lights dimmed for the drama of the long struggle between the two men which was to plunge the monarchy and the "constitutional question" of the king's powers into the political arena until they became the chief cause of dispute between political parties for many years and finally affected the whole of Greece's political life.

Venizelos claimed that King Constantine I had exceeded his constitutional powers by dismissing a prime minister under the existing circumstances. Under the constitution of 1864 and its modifications in 1911, the king was given lifelong and hereditary tenure but was to exercise "no other powers than those explicitly conferred upon him by the constitution and the special laws made in pursuance thereto."[7] But neither constitution nor laws made it entirely clear whether the king in the exercise of his undeniable right to appoint and dismiss ministers had the power to dismiss a prime minister who had a majority in Parliament, and to compound the difficulty by doing the same thing twice in the same year, and after an election reaffirming the majority. The struggle this precipitated was to continue through future years and future constitutions and end in a tragedy which began in 1965 and came to its climax in 1967.

End of First Reign of Constantine I, 1917

Both Venizelos and the Allies strongly opposed the King's policies concerning the war. In Thessaloniki, Venizelos organized his own government, which declared war on Bulgaria and Germany, while the King remained in Athens with his supporters and government. Tired of Constantine's unwillingness to join them, the Allies demanded his abdication. In response to this pressure and to the unpopularity of his policies at home, the King left Greece in 1917, two years after the Allied landings in Thessaloniki, but did not formally abdicate. He took with him his eldest son, Crown Prince George, who in the Allied view was tarred with the same German brush as his father.

Brief Reign of King Alexander, 1917–1920, and Return of Constantine I, 1920

Before leaving Greece, Constantine appointed his second son, Alexander, to succeed him. Fatally bitten while playing in his garden with two pet monkeys, King Alexander reigned only three years. With the refusal of the throne by Alexander's younger brother, Paul, Greece was faced with the alternatives of recalling Constantine, finding another king, or abolishing the monarchy. In a plebiscite held in November 1920, all but a fraction of the more than one million Greeks who voted chose the recall of Constantine I. Amid great acclaim, the King returned after approximately three years of exile. But the Allies refused to recognize him and withdrew their support from his country.

King Constantine was not destined to remain long on the throne. Nor did Venizelos fare any better than the king he had opposed. In elections held the same month as the plebiscite, he and his party were so badly defeated at the polls that he left the country, to be gone for eight years. As leader in promoting the "Great Idea," he had favored Greece's retention of territorial gains promised under the Treaty of Sèvres. So many Greeks were tired of long years of war that votes poured in against a stand which had been responsible in large part for Greece's undertaking of the tragic military campaign in Asia Minor. Other Greeks blamed Venizelos and the Allies for not backing the attempt as they had been expected to do. Many others, including members of the army and a large number of the vast throng of refugees pouring into Greece from Turkey, found in King Constantine their scapegoat for the disaster. He had not, however, taken part in the actual decision to embark in the war, or in its military direction.

Military Coup and Revolutionary Government of Colonel Plastiras, 1922

In the deeply demoralized Greek army after its defeat in Asia Minor in September 1922, one group of officers, led by Colonel (later General) Nikolaos Plastiras, was particularly anxious for vindication and a scapegoat. They had fled from the coast of Asia Minor to the not-far-distant island of Chios. There they issued an ultimatum: the King must abdicate or else they would march on Athens with a sizable army and take forcible measures against those responsible for the defeat. Although the King still retained the loyalty of a number of troops, he decided that he was unwilling to bring about civil war in a defeated and weakened Greece, and so he abdicated.

After the King had left the throne and Colonel Plastiras

and his men arrived in Athens, his officers appointed a revolutionary committee, which in turn set up a commission of inquiry to allocate the blame for the Asia minor débâcle. After vainly attempting to find a civilian willing to become prime minister, the revolutionary officers appointed one, and formed a cabinet, from among their own number. Meanwhile, a court martial of eleven officers tried and found guilty six of King Constantine's leading advisers, including his prime minister and the commander-in-chief of the army.

The English and the Italian ministers in Athens protested the trial, and when the men were shot, England broke off diplomatic relations with Greece. The whole tragic story of the execution of the six, only two of whom had been strongly opposed to Constantine, had world-wide repercussions which took the country long to outlive. Not until 1924 was a constitutional regime re-established. It was easier then, as it turned out to be later, for the nation to turn to dictatorship than to recover from its effects.

King George II on the Throne for the First Time, 1922–1924

Before leaving Greece, King Constantine I handed the succession over to his eldest son, George, who had been excluded as a possibility by the Allies only two years earlier. The new king, George II, ruled little more than a year after his coronation before the institution of the monarchy had become such a source of friction that the King, without formally abdicating, was persuaded to leave Greece for what was thought would be a short time to allow political passions to cool. They did not cool easily, however, and the King's exile lasted from 1924 until 1935.

The Second Republic of Modern Greece, 1924–1935

One of the chief reasons King George II left his throne was the activity of a group of discontented, comparatively young officers of the armed forces who had become active republicans and formed a Republican Officers' League.

With the support of the League, a republic was proclaimed on March 24, 1924, and confirmed by plebiscite soon afterwards. Others than republicans favored the change because they hoped that a republic might prove the way to attain internal stability and peace in a nation torn asunder by political rivalries. The birth of the republic, nevertheless, came generally as a surprise. Despite the constant arguments over the monarchy among the political parties, no strong tradition of opposition to a monarchy had grown up among the Greek people during their years of national life, nor had any serious preference for a republic appeared to be generally widespread.

The republic proved to be no less subject to political crises and changes of government than the monarchy had been. Discontent was rife again over both internal and external affairs as well as over the form of government. Finally political chaos became so great that the military forces again took it upon themselves to deal with it.

Military Coup and Brief Dictatorship of General Pangalos, 1926

This time it was the higher officers of the armed forces who instigated the upheaval. At the beginning of 1926, General Theodoros Pangalos, chief of the army staff and leader of the Republican Officers' League, secured the backing of the commanding admiral of the navy and suddenly seized power, announcing that elections fixed for January 10 were indefinitely postponed, and that all executive and administrative power was transferred to him because of the need for restoring political peace and improvement in the economy of the country. Although he had no particular political belief which he was anxious to have his countrymen accept, General Pangalos soon established a dictatorship which he believed would end political wrangling and provide the nation with stable administration.

Exiling various political opponents to the islands, Pangalos also subjected the press to such strict censorship as effectively to kill all expressions of public opinion. Of all his actions, however, the one most often remembered was a measure forbidding women's skirts to be more than fourteen inches from the ground.[8] Dictatorships are often prone to puritanism.

Slightly more than two months after assuming power, General Pangalos announced that the constitution for the republic would be ready within about six more weeks and that it would strengthen the powers of the president. But preparation for the constitution dragged, and events moved more rapidly than progress. In an election in which arrangements for voting were completed in only a small number of districts, Pangalos was the only candidate and he not unnaturally was made president of the republic. His days in office, however, were numbered. In August 1926 he was overthrown in another bloodless coup and was then imprisoned. General Georgios Kondylis, the leader of the coup, had no intention of becoming a dictator, and he and his followers refused to run for office in elections held the following autumn. When the elections failed to give the republicans enough votes to enable them to form a united cabinet a coalition was formed, consisting of monarchists and royalists as well as republicans. But its disagreements were so many that little progress was made, and not until the following year was a constitution finally agreed on for the republic, already three years old. It tottered on shaky feet.

General Pangalos was a military man who had taken over power for political ends. Despite what was reported to be a certain benevolence in his nature, Pangalos ruled by force and lacked the qualities of a leader.[9] He "failed as a dictator because he proved unable to deal successfully with the internal troubles of the country, and had performed no services which could win the gratitude or the admiration, or even the confidence of the nation . . . there were no outstanding questions of international relations which could not be solved by peaceful means. . . . A dictator may often prolong his rule by military successes which flatter the *amour propre* of his people; but the situation offered no scope for achievements of this kind. . . . Finally, there is in Greece no tradition of discipline and blind obedience, and there was no external threat to induce the people to subject themselves to the will of an irresponsible ruler, whose efforts were directed to putting an end to their chief amusement in life, the game of party politics."[10]

Only two years after the overthrow of Pangalos, parliamentary government received a new lease on life with the return of Eleutherios Venizelos to active political life and to the leadership of the Liberal Party. Within a few months after his return he had again become prime minister, forming a government which was supported by two-thirds of Parliament. Even with such strong support, he was less than successful with his formation of a Senate under the Constitution of 1927, for the idea of two chambers had little appeal. Nor was he able to lower taxes. His important accomplishments were in the field of foreign policy. During more than four years in power, he brought about radical changes in its orientation, including reconciliation with Turkey and settlement of outstanding questions between Greece and Italy and Greece and Yugoslavia. But even his program in relation to Turkey brought him royalist opposition.

Attempted Military Coups, 1933 and 1935

The return to parliamentary government after the fall of Pangalos failed to strengthen the republic. To try to prevent its overthrow and especially to prevent the loss of their military commands, inevitable if a monarchy were restored, a group of ardent republican officers, believing that the republic was being undermined by the royalists, determined to try to uphold it. There was doubtless justice in their claim. Under the nominal leadership of the same General Nikolaos Plastiras who had engineered the 1922 revolt, a number of officers tried to seize power in 1933 and again in 1935. The 1933 effort was not completed, in part at least because Venizelos told Plastiras that he considered it unwise to try a dictatorship. "If you become dictator," he told Plastiras on the night of the election, "you will fail dismally within three months, because you will be unable to solve any of the economic problems which are uppermost in our minds."[11] Economic problems there were—world-wide depression, unemployment within Greece, inflation, the poverty-stricken people of the underdeveloped economy. But these were not the cause of the attempted coup. An undeveloped political structure based on foreign models and a citizenry lacking in civic training and experience were more basic reasons.

In the second and more important attempt at military takeover the officers occupied various army installations. Then the cruiser *Averoff* and a few smaller ships joined the uprising briefly, and Venizelos himself suddenly took part in the movement. It attracted no great support among the general public or the majority of the armed forces, and the officers on the mainland for the most part were overpowered and the warships forced to surrender. Venizelos retired to Rhodes and then to Paris.

In another of the many moves in modern Greek history to try to keep the military forces out of politics, purges in the army and changes in the civil service followed hard on the heels of the attempted coups. A large number of army officers were removed, and professors and teachers were dismissed from their posts. One of the officers was condemned by a court-martial and put to death, while both Venizelos and Plastiras were condemned to death in their providential absence from the country. These severe measures caused international repercussions and brought protests and requests from other countries to lessen the severity. The army and navy, however, were deeply entrenched in the political soil of Greece, and the protests accomplished little.

George II on the Throne Again, 1935

Despite the constant political upheaval of the republic, it still had numerous sympathizers throughout the country. The monarchists, however, obtained the upper hand in Parliament, not only because of their pressure for the King's return but also because the leading republican political groups refused to take part in elections held in June 1935. With control of Parliament, the monarchists were in a position to move ahead. Some were impatient and unwilling to wait until the real views of the people became clear. The prime minister, Panagis Tsaldaris, however, favored the King's return but insisted that it must come in response to a fairly conducted referendum. Before a plebiscite had been arranged, in still another interference of army officers in politics, high-ranking officers of the three branches of the military forces held up the prime minister's car on the road between Athens and its lovely suburb Kifissia, and forced him to resign his office. Behind the move, it was generally believed, was the hand of the man who would be the next prime minister, General Georgios Kondylis.

Less than a month later, the plebiscite was held. In it restoration of the monarchy was given so large a majority—approximately 97 per cent of the votes cast—that its very size raised the question, especially among the republicans, of the possible falsification of the returns. But the majority did at least show that the pendulum of popularity had swung back to the monarchy.

After more than eleven years' absence from the throne, George II returned to Greece as king at the end of 1935. Before his death in 1936, even Eleutherios Venizelos, weary of his long feud with King Constantine's family, and by then fearing that there would be no other way to unity than through a monarchy, expressed his belief in the wisdom of King George II's return.

The King remained on the throne and stayed in Athens throughout the years from 1936 to 1941, in which time parliamentary government was abolished and Greece was governed by a strong and able dictator. The King appeared powerless to influence the course of the dictatorship, and his inaction was held against him by many people for the rest of his life. But the institution of the monarchy remained, enduring even through the bitter years of war and guerrilla fighting which were ahead.

CHAPTER 5

Parliaments, Political Parties, and the Long Dictatorship before World War II

Like the monarchy, the system of Greek constitutional parliamentary government came into being in response to factors both within and outside the country. Although the constitutions of the War of Independence and of Troizin showed Greek interest in the principle of representative government, the background for the adoption of that principle in Greece was more truly foreign. The idea took root slowly in Greece because of lack of geographical homogeneity, the desire of the separate and rival insurrectionary leaders to retain power for themselves, the individualism of the Greeks, and the dominating interests of the three protecting powers.

Seventeen years and a coup d'état came between the founding of the nation and creation of the assembly of 1844 as modern Greece's first legislative body. Even so, it was established with the grudging consent of King Othon, forced by the coup of the preceding year, and the essence of the monarchy remained absolute. Under the constitution of 1844 and the assembly it set up, nevertheless, the first steps toward representative government were taken and the foundations for political division were strengthened. Although the protecting powers still had a voice in Greek affairs when the next constitution was adopted in 1864 and a more truly representative parliament set up, that year may be said to have marked the birth of constitutional parliamentary government in Greece, for no longer were the important powers centered in the person of the king.

In view of recent experience with the continuation of King Othon's absolute control, the document of 1864 took care to make it clear that the people and not the king alone were henceforward to be the real source of authority. He was given lifelong and hereditary tenure but "exercised no other powers than those explicitly conferred upon him by the Constitution and the special laws made in pursuance thereto; all powers are derived from the nation and are exercised in a manner prescribed by the Constitution."[1] Although an integral part of the legislative process, the monarch could exercise legislative powers only through his cabinet ministers. As in later constitutions, the personal influence of the sovereign was granted no constitutional place, and "any arbitrary interference by the Crown in the affairs of the nation was the negation of the essential principles of democracy; the will of the people expressed through their elected representatives was the only source of power in the State."[2]

As a reaction from the two-chambered Parliament of 1844, the new Assembly consisted of only one house, chosen by direct, secret, and universal suffrage, although the word "universal" was still given a somewhat restricted meaning. In a hope to lessen sectional rivalry, the constitution provided that deputies were elected to represent the nation and not the districts from which they were chosen. The number of chambers was later changed to two, and again back to one, as it remained under the constitution of 1952. Under that constitution, Parliament consisted of 300 deputies, a number that varied up and down over the years. But in general the principles of the constitution of 1864 were little changed in the document of 1952.

Origin of Political Parties

It took a legislative organization to bring about the flowering of political parties. The early division of Greek political currents had come about because of the presence of English, French, and Russian interest, and because a particular leader or chieftain had followed the leadership of one of the three powers while his opponents or enemies followed the others.[3] Thus Capodistrias had been made president of the republic because of the interest of the important "Russian party."

With the establishment of the 1844 Parliament, parties began to assume a somewhat less inchoate shape, but were still based on English, French, or Russian interest. In that year the prime minister was Alexander Mavrocordato, a leading statesman connected with the "English" party; he was followed in office by Ioannis Kolettis of the "French" party. The differences between the two men consisted of disagreements over priority rather than policy or principle. They failed to agree as to whether the nation at that time should confine itself solely to its numerous internal problems or expend its chief energies on the attempt to take in other territories and other people of Greek background.

Orientation of political parties on such bases gave them a false start and provided another cause of disillusionment with politics to add to those remaining from the days of foreign occupation. From these early seeds were to spring later distrust of foreign interest in Greece.

The Monarchy and the Kaleidoscope of Party Politics before 1936

For many years there was one important issue in political life, the "constitutional question" of the monarchy in all its

manifold shadings. Political parties played different variations of the same theme, and often they were so alike that
even an expert could just barely see that the tunes differed
at all. The long and tortured story of the early political
parties not only is a volume in itself but also has been told
elsewhere.[4] It is enough to say here that the numerous divisions which became endemic in Greek politics were precipitated, if they were not caused, by the long-drawn-out feud
between King Constantine I and his prime minister, Eleutherios Venizelos.

From this feud and the differences in personalities arose
the two parties which were the chief protagonists in the
political drama until 1936, when all political organizations
were banned. It was not until after World War II that
parliamentary government was resumed again, and then the
same parties reappeared. Although party names and leaders
changed with time, their bases were destined to continue.

The first of the two was the Liberal Party (*Komma Phile-
leftheron,* KP), led by Venizelos for most of the time after
his arrival in Athens and first appointment as prime minister
in 1910 until his death in 1936; the other was the Populist
or Popular Party (*Laikon Komma,* LK) under a succession
of leaders. The Populists were generally thought of as promonarchist and the Liberals as prorepublican, but the facts
did not entirely bear out this belief. Although Venizelos
had his republican moments, in the long run he was in favor
of a king with limited powers who reigned rather than ruled.
As long as Venizelos was the moving Liberal spirit, the
Populists were more anti-Venizelos than promonarchist.
Despite their espousal of a democratic monarchy, republicans
and monarchists alike were found in both parties, and differences centered primarily in the personalities of the leaders.

Around the Liberals and the Populists buzzed a swarm of

small parties of varying shades and minor degrees of differ-
entiation over the ever-recurring argument concerning the
monarchy and the powers of the king. For many years
the small Republican Party was the most important among the
group. Strongly favoring a republic, it acted as a gadfly to both
Liberals and Populists. Although the Communists emerged
as a small political organization just before the 1920s, they
turned out to be in a class by themselves.

Personal Nature of Politics

Greek politics and political parties have always been exceedingly personal, depending on allegiances to men rather
than to ideologies or issues. While the individualism of the
Greeks made every voter appear to be a "one-man splinter
group," the family system and the traditional loyalties and
close ties forming part of it encouraged people to follow the
political leadership of someone to whom they were related or
with whom they had been closely associated in their native
villages. As a result, political leaders and parties became so
numerous that a casual observer might well have thought
them to be as many as the Greeks themselves. All too frequently, the history of Parliaments was written in terms of
initials of so many political groups as to appear a veritable
labyrinth of political symbols.

A candidate for election as deputy was likely to be nominated chiefly as a result of some such close association and
not as the result of interplay between national and local politics and party headquarters. The administration of government was too highly centralized for local organizations to
become truly important on the national scene. Once elected,
a deputy found it easy to refuse to accept party decisions or
to support them on major policies in Parliament, as is true

in any country where strong party discipline has not developed. In Greece, the individualism of the deputies meant so great a lack of party discipline that ministers often were unable to find the support necessary to govern. The Greeks, therefore, cynical and almost unperturbed, appeared to accept the fall of a government as normal, whatever parliamentary government was in power.

Disagreements over personalities or shadings of personal opinion sometimes caused parties to disintegrate entirely. Leaders frequently moved from one party to another or founded still a different group. New political organizations therefore often became only regroupings of old forces under new names. In periods of instability, when governments came and went with great rapidity, such shifts were continuous; when stable governments were the rule, regroupings of new parties were less frequent. But the currents of instability still existed underneath, and the wine of old parties was constantly decanted and poured into old bottles with new labels. Such splits and divisions were symptoms of still further disillusionment with the political process, and continued to be so in the years after World War II.

Prime Ministers and Parliaments

Political party loyalties and shifts were nowhere more apparent than in the party relationship to a prime minister. As in the English system, the prime minister and his cabinet constituted "the government," which stood or fell according to a vote of confidence, or of no-confidence, in Parliament.

If deputies willing to work in a cabinet could not be found within a prime minister's own party or in parties willing to cooperate with him, he was permitted to go outside Parliament to find candidates. The road to political preferment thus became smooth; a minister so appointed did not have to be elected to Parliament first and so was not responsible directly to the electorate as he is in England. The practice of appointing extra-parliamentary ministers was used frequently and with disastrous results by King Othon and by King George I in the early years of his reign.

When a government failed to secure a vote of confidence, the king was able to appoint one prime minister after another until a candidate was found with enough support to pass the parliamentary muster. If no prime minister selected by a monarch was able to secure the necessary parliamentary backing, the king had the power to dissolve Parliament and call new elections. But he was not *required* to issue the decree of dissolution. The matter lay in his discretion.

During his career in Parliament, a prime minister could try to steer among political shoals by asking for another vote of confidence to indicate agreement of the deputies—or lack of it—with his position on a given matter. Usually on a proposal by the opposition parties, Parliament was able to initiate a vote of no-confidence. Even without such a vote, a prime minister who had lost his majority resigned so that the Crown might exercise its right of dissolution and give the electorate a chance to pronounce its verdict at a new election. It was also possible for a prime minister in command of a majority to submit his resignation to the king on his own initiative and so sound out the feelings of the electorate at a given time.

If a major party failed to elect enough members to secure control of Parliament, a government could be formed by a coalition of parties, even without possibility of united opinion among its parts. Although sometimes tried, a minority government was a weak alternative, seldom if ever able to survive long enough to carry through a whole program. Usually a prime minister chosen by the king from the largest party in Parliament went around, tin cup in hand, begging cooperation from leaders of other parties. Nevertheless, he always had to pay a price for their aid. Coalitions were always inherently explosive and were likely to disintegrate sooner rather than later.

When it proved impossible to find a formula by which to constitute a government, the dissolution of Parliament followed. Then came new elections, appointment of a new prime minister, and another attempt—or attempts—to form a government which could maneuver itself through. As the system provided no certainty of political survival to the end of an election period, shifts of political power were likely to be numerous. Then the electorate frequently grew restless, fears of disorder grew, and the possibility loomed large of takeover by military forces or by a dictatorship.

Voting Mechanics, a Determining Factor in Elections

The mechanics of voting were often almost as important as personalities in determining the number of deputies each political party could elect to Parliament and in the role each party could play after election. There was frequently a bitter struggle when a Parliament decided the method of voting to be used in a forthcoming election. The choice of election type was between majority vote and proportional representation, either simple or with some variation. Under a system of majority voting, a candidate was elected when he secured the majority of all the votes cast; a small plurality could carry one single election district, and even a sizable vote for another candidate in that same district got no rewards in the final outcome. Under proportional representation every vote counted toward election and even minute groups were assured representation in accordance with the size of their voting returns. A Parliament so constituted often consisted of a congeries of small, warring groups and their leaders, with more than the usual amount of log-rolling among them.

The majority system was usually preferred by a party, no matter what its political complexion, which believed it could elect a candidate in a given district by even a small plurality. In that case its opponents would get no representation in that district. When eager to divide the vote of its strongest rival and so strengthen its own position, a party preferred proportional representation. In an attempt to get the best of all possible worlds, it sometimes chose proportional representation "reinforced" or "modified" in one way or another to get some of the advantages of the majority system.

Although the major parties usually found that the majority system gave them the greatest gains in seats, this was not always so. The Populists and the Liberals both found occasions when they were closely matched in strength and when proportional representation suited their purposes better. In such circumstances each party hoped that balloting by proportional representation might disperse the votes of the other among the smaller groups and so lessen its possibility of winning many seats. In another situation, a formerly strong party preferred to use proportional representation which would allow it to cling to at least a few seats.

The most serious effects of the use of proportional representation became clear when the votes were so scattered that no party could obtain a majority. In that case a small party without an impressive vote was able to secure the balance of legislative power and so could trade with the largest groups to get what it wanted. The small party in that position usually turned out to be the Communist.

Various elections held from 1926 to 1935 illustrate the

difficulty. The first was held in 1926 after General Georgios Kondylis overthrew the Pangalos dictatorship. The General decided to hold elections in November of that year, to be conducted under rules of proportional representation. The scales were evenly balanced between the Liberals and the Populists, and as either one might win, both agreed to the use of proportional representation. As was to be expected, the vote was divided so that neither major party secured a majority of the seats. The largest number went to the Liberals because the republic was still young and hopeful, and more of them were likely to favor its continuation and success than the Populists. But for the first time the Communist-backed Popular Front had entered the lists. Winning just under 42,000 votes and ten out of the total of 286 seats, it was able, together with the other small parties, to secure a strong bargaining position.[5]

In the serious political difficulties of the republic in the summer of 1928, when it was limping along under a coalition cabinet of men of widely divergent political beliefs, Venizelos came back into political life from which he had been absent for eight years. He was the only leader strong enough to form a united government, and under the circumstances he believed only a return to a majority system of voting could accomplish the necessary end. Venizelos accordingly persuaded the president of the republic, Admiral Koundouriotis, to abolish proportional representation by decree. As a result of the use of the majority system of voting and because of faith in Venizelos, the elections resulted in strong backing for his government, which secured the support of two-thirds of the deputies in Parliament.

With the hours of the republic running out in 1933, the machinery of voting had an even more decisive effect on the outcome of elections held on March 5 of that year under the majority system. The Populist vote was large enough to be the precipitating force for the republican coup of Colonel Plastiras. This occurred dramatically on election day evening as soon as reports from a number of election districts had shown which way the wind was blowing. The Liberals came in second in the race, and the Popular Front, with a vote of somewhat more than 52,000 out of a total of 1,141,331— almost as many as they had secured in elections the preceding September when the voting had been by proportional representation—got no seats because of the majority system of voting.[6]

In the last days of the weakened republic in 1935, the method of voting was again a determining factor in the election outcome and in the position of the Communist-dominated Popular Front at the outcome. There was no doubt that the issue was clear: Did the nation want a return to a monarchy or not? The monarchists made strenuous efforts to bring about the return, and, in addition, there was a wave of reaction against the Liberal Party and any other party with a republican slant. They had lost both face and support because of the unsuccessful outcome of the republican seizure of the cruiser *Averoff*, the attempted republican coup, and the subsequent departure of Venizelos. The only hope for the Liberals would have been in elections by proportional representation by which they would have secured at least some seats. As the majority method was chosen, the Liberals and other republicans abstained from the elections. Their abstention, however, did not materially lessen the large vote. The Populists secured a high count and, although the Popular Front got almost 99,000 votes, none of its candidates was elected because of the operation of the majority system.[7] Although the Communists were still "a small though boisterous force, operating on the periphery of national life,"[8] their numbers were clearly growing.

The return of King George II in November of that year

did not settle feelings about the monarchy, and the ferris wheel of political parties continued to turn around it. The myriad shadings of monarchist and republican belief still existed, and political parties continued to be formed on grounds of only minute differences on the subject of the crown and its powers.

With so many political parties having such small differences among them, only a miracle could have made one political group the decisive victor in the elections held in January 1936, the year after the return of King George II to the throne. The possibility of any miracle was effectively prevented by the use of proportional representation, agreed to by both Liberals and Populists. The Populists and several minor monarchist parties secured the largest number of seats; the Liberals, running in conjunction with a group of small, not very dissimilar parties, came in a close second. Neither Populists nor Liberals with their respective followers had received a majority, and so neither could form a government. It was the old dilemma again. The Communist-backed Popular Front, with a vote of slightly under 74,000 out of the total of nearly 1,300,000 votes cast, elected only a small number of deputies, but enough to give them the balance of power in Parliament as they first had ten years earlier.[9] They thus secured more power than their actual vote would indicate.

After the elections, the major parties had the choice of abandoning their disputes long enough to set up a coalition government or turning to the Communists for support in Parliament. Unable to agree sufficiently to work together, the Liberals and the Populists each made secret contacts with the Popular Front to secure its backing and the Liberals went so far as to enter an agreement with it. Finally realizing how much under the Communist thumb his party would be, the Liberal leader, Themistoklis Sofoulis, changed his mind about

the agreement and refused to accept the office of prime minister because a vote of confidence dependent on the support
of the Communists would have meant that the Liberals had
given in to them.

The Communist Party, 1918–1936

By 1936 the Communists had become a factor to be reck-
oned with in political life. For all their small size as a party,
they had shown great adeptness at seizing opportunities to
cement their position as a chief bargainer in Parliament.
People began to look into them and their history.

The origins of the Greek Communist party organization
went back to days before the Russian Revolution when a
number of adherents of the Socialist Party of Greece (*Sosialistikon Komma Ellados,* EKS) came to be ideologically
on its left flank. They were a group of unrealistic intellectuals
and idealists fervently interested in the promotion of social
justice. Disputes raged among them over matters of theory as
well as over personalities. In 1918 the Russian Revolution
inspired them to try to become a more cohesive group with
a life and organization of its own, and they organized themselves as the Greek Socialist Labor Party (*Sosialistikon
Ergatikon Komma Ellados,* SEK). Recognized by the Comintern in 1920, this faction changed its name four years later
to the Communist Party of Greece (*Kommunistikon Komma
Ellados,* KKE).

For approximately the first fifteen years of its existence,
the group remained small and unimportant. Its own official
count showed that two years after its organization, the KKE
had no more than 2,500 members.[10] At that time there appeared no reason for the party to try to hide its size. The
KKE at first appealed only to a few of the middle-class

intellectuals of the cities and towns. Later a few low-paid workers in the tobacco industry were persuaded that Communism would improve their lot, although they had no idea what Communism meant or what the Russian experience signified. Gradually some of the ethnic minorities, especially in Macedonia, victims of the discontent long prevalent among the various Balkan peoples, were persuaded to enter the Communist ranks in the vague hope of achieving an independent Macedonia. Some of the refugees from Anatolia were added to the number, together with others from the Black Sea area of the U.S.S.R., uprooted psychologically as well as physically, living in overcrowded homes without work or outlets.

Slowly the Communists made conquests among the industrial workers and particularly in Thessaloniki, which, as the capital of Macedonia and one of the earliest and most important of the industrial cities of Greece, became a stronghold of Leftist agitation. But throughout Greece before World War II industry was merely on the fringes of development, the number of industrial employees was small, and they continued to maintain a "peasant outlook" on life, with no conception of what uniting "the workers of the world" meant. It was not until the mid-1930s that the Communists successfully pushed any of the industrial workers into riots and disturbances of importance.

Despite the preponderance of poor farmers among the Greeks in the years after the party was founded, Communism made no real headway in the countryside; most of its supporters were still found in the cities and larger towns. Of all individualistic Greeks, the farm workers are among the most notably so. They found little appeal in the idea of collective farming, particularly as the land reform of that era had increased the number of small farmers deeply attached to their own bits of land, no matter how tiny.

The doctrine that religion is "the opiate of the people" made little headway among the Orthodox Greeks. Nor as intense nationalists did they take to the idea of an independent Macedonia, composed of Slavs and Greeks, which the Communists advocated so strongly. In general, Communist ideology found little ready response in the Greece of the 1920s and 1930s.

For the first years of its life as a political party, the Communist organization made slow progress at the polls, securing usually under 10 per cent of the total vote. Some of the party members and leaders did not believe in working through the ballot, but once the decision to go ahead had been taken they were disappointed by the results. Such headway as the party was able to make was due less to the fire of its propaganda than to the constant feud between the Populists and the Liberals and the continued divisions within each party organization. Even when their popular vote increased and when elections were carried on by majority ballot, the Communists failed to elect any deputies because of heavy concentration of the Communists in certain localities and in cities such as Thessaloniki. When voting was conducted by proportional representation and every vote counted, even the smallest groups were sometimes able to secure a few seats, and some Communist candidates were usually elected. When the major parties were evenly balanced, the Communists were often able to emerge with the balance of power in Parliament.

The Communists took their first significant strides in 1926, primarily because they were able to win more votes from patriotic Greeks, especially in Macedonia, as the party had dropped its controversial demand for Macedonian independence, including the possibility of entire separation of a Macedonian state from Greece. In the elections of 1928, despite the passage of only two years, a Communist decline set in, much influenced by the return of confidence to other parties after Venizelos had come back as prime minister that year. The Communist candidates secured only somewhat over 14,000 votes out of a total of more than a million cast. As a result of the majority system of voting their small vote gave them no representation in Parliament.

In the early 1930s economic depression swept away Greek economic strength which had grown in the first two years after Venizelos' return as prime minister. Unrest rose as the poor were more unable than ever to meet their bills, and the first months of 1932 brought about a series of strikes against economic ills, and began to strengthen Communist influence. Their vote of over 52,000 in the 1933 elections carried on under the majority system was almost as large as they had secured in the elections of the preceding September under the system of proportional representation, when they knew that every vote they cast would count for their candidates.

Throughout their history the Communists failed to form a truly united and coherent party. Even after their early success in 1926 the party ranks showed an immediate split. Among their ten Communist deputies, only one was pro-Stalinist, and the party leaders of that faction outside Parliament precipitated dissension in it because of their anxiety to unseat the other nine. The split was symptomatic of future disagreements. Within the party ranks the pendulum was destined always to swing back and forth between those who believed in seizing power by force and violence and those who thought infiltration by clandestine means and by political action would bring greater gains.

Nikos Zakhariades and Georgios Siantos, Communist Leaders

The dominant figure in Greek Communist circles in the decade of the 1930s was Nikolaos (Nikos) Zakhariades, by both temperament and training a believer in the overthrow of the existing order by violent means. For a few years, he was succeeded by Georgios Siantos, a man of opposite beliefs and methods of operation.

Zakhariades' background and youth had the greatest influence on his future political orientation. Born in 1902 in Nicomedia in Asia Minor, he left Turkey among the flood of refugees of the early 1920s. Going to Moscow in 1922, Zakhariades graduated from the Communist Party training school for eastern peoples. Three years later, he was sent to Greece, where he joined the Communist organization of Thessaloniki. Imprisoned for advocating Macedonian independence, Zakhariades went back to the U.S.S.R. on his release.

In 1931 the Comintern appointed Zakhariades party leader of the Greek Communist Party, and four years later he was given the newly created post of Secretary General of the Greek party. With "an unswerving devotion to the cause of Communism, [he was] ambitious and intelligent, with a passion for organization and secrecy, a winning personality with a hot temper, he was the man to take over the leadership of the disjointed party."[11] Elected as a deputy in 1936, he was soon imprisoned again and remained there until after the Germans entered Greece, when he was sent from his Greek cell to the concentration camp at Dachau. There he miraculously survived. But Zakhariades had spent so much of his life outside of Greece and so much time in Greece within prison walls that he remained out of touch with the trends in Greek Communist thinking for long periods.

In the meanwhile, Georgios Siantos, a man much more truly Greek in background, had come to the front of the party. Born in Karthisa in 1890, Siantos was the son of a poor family of tobacco workers. Starting to work in the fields at an early age, he was never educated beyond the fourth grade of elementary school. He later enrolled in the Communist-run tobacco workers union and joined the party itself in 1920. Like Zakhariades, he was arrested but was exiled to one of the islands instead of being sent to prison.

From 1937 until 1941, Siantos' history was one of repeated arrests and repeated hairbreadth escapes. In 1942 he was elected Secretary of the Central Committee of the Communist Party of Greece and so was in a position to affect party policy during the crucial early days of World War II. Unlike Zakhariades, Siantos advocated the soft strategy of political action rather than violent overthrow of the existing order. Disagreements between the two men went on all of their political lives. Among the Communists as well as in the other parties, differences of personality were a crucial issue.

Dictatorship of General Metaxas and Abolition of Parliamentary Government, 1936–1940

After the elections which had been held in January 1936, political wrangling among all the parties and leaders occupied the rest of the first three months of that year. As no coalition of parties appeared able to form a lasting government, a non-party man, Constantine Demertzis, was persuaded to become prime minister and form a coalition government, with General Ioannis Metaxas as his deputy and minister of war. When the Prime Minister died before he was able to appear in Parliament, Metaxas, next in line for the office, took over. He secured an overwhelming vote of confidence at the end of April of that year. Without fanfare, without military take-over, he came into power by constitutional means, and with the votes in Parliament of those who were tired of the whirligig.

General Metaxas, however, was no believer in the give and take of representative government. Coming into prominence as an able staff officer in the Balkan Wars, he was a military strategist by inclination and training. Serving as military and political adviser to King Constantine I, he had opposed Greek cooperation with the Allies in their attack on the Dardanelles in World War I, and was widely regarded as pro-German. After the success of the Venizelos pro-Allied policy in Greece and the entry of Allied troops into Thessaloniki, Metaxas was exiled and went to live in Corsica. Later returning to Greece, he organized a pro-royalist coup at the time of republican demonstrations and rioting in 1923, but his attempt boomeranged and even helped stimulate the growth of republican sentiment. Although later elected to Parliament, Metaxas still distrusted its possibilities for governing the country.

Before he obtained the vote of confidence in Parliament, Metaxas already believed that the never-ending jockeying for position by the political parties made government impossible. He secured the immediate consent of Parliament to its own adjournment for a period of five months and at the same time was given the power to govern by decree during that period, subject only to the approval of a politically constituted parliamentary committee.

To Metaxas, as to many others, the nation appeared to be on the verge of a revolution by the Communists. While controlling the balance of power in Parliament, they had been active in fomenting serious disorders throughout the country, especially among the industrial workers. In Thessaloniki, for example, where Communism had long since made considerable headway, a strike assumed such proportions as to have caused bloodshed. When a general strike was called four months after Metaxas took office, he persuaded King George II to sign decrees dissolving Parliament, banning political parties, instituting martial law, and suspending civil liberties guaranteed by the constitution.

He abolished freedom of the press, allowed censorship of even some of the Greek classical dramas and Pericles' orations, and sent various of his opponents to the islands, forbidding them to return. Soon Republicans and Communists alike were exiled or imprisoned, others fled or retired to private life. All political parties and their leaders disappeared from the scene. The Communist party organization broke down, and many of its members deserted the cause, even going so far as to make a complete turnabout to follow Metaxas. The roots of the Communist movement nevertheless continued underground. Although without legal entity, the Communists carried on what they deemed their most important work of digging deep into the foundations of the trade union and cooperative movements. Some fled to the Balkan countries to the north and remained there after the outbreak of World War II. When those countries became Communist, these men had a head start on the military and propaganda training which the disciplined party organizations offered in those countries.

In economic matters, until the outbreak of World War II in 1939, Metaxas had turned more and more to Germany for trade. Although declaring himself ready to buy needed goods from England, he bought them from Germany, forced to do so by the need for the funds available from unused credits of agricultural contracts between Germany and Greece made during the depression years. He withstood heavy pressure from the Axis powers to repudiate the Anglo-French guarantees while attempting not to be provocative towards Berlin and Rome. But the impression continued for some time that he was favorable to Germany.

Despite his introduction of social insurance, minimum wages, and maternity and child welfare legislation, Metaxas was not generally popular with the liberty-loving Greeks. Somehow the signs extolling his accomplishments which the authors saw in Athens the latter part of the 1930s had a hollow look. Discouraged though the Greeks may have been with the political situation before Metaxas became prime minister, they found the government which he instituted one of little appeal. He was tolerated because threats of war were issuing from Mussolini and Hitler in those years, and "the Greeks knew that it was not easy for them to combine political liberties with unity in the face of danger from authoritarian neighbors."[12] But judgments on Metaxas were softened after the Italians suddenly invaded the country and he courageously ordered the Greek army to stand against them. Metaxas died less than three months before the German invasion brought the full holocaust of calamity to Greece, and so he never knew the full extent of the horrors which the Axis powers were to pile on his country.

CHAPTER 6

The Dreadful Decade, 1940–1950

For ten crucial years after the dissolution of Parliament in 1936, Greece had no representative governmental institutions. After the dictatorship had lasted four years, the sudden invasion of the Axis powers brought war and occupation to Greece, and only the courage of the people enabled them to survive the years of struggle. From 1940 until 1944 the country was prostrated by warfare and occupation, first by Italy and then Germany and Bulgaria. Then after peace had come to Western Europe, Greece was again stricken, this time by a bitter Communist invasion, by insurrection, and by civil warfare which lasted until the Communists were finally defeated on the field of battle in 1949. In human losses the four-year guerrilla fighting cost more than the struggle against the Axis powers. As a result of the guerrilla warfare, Greek thinking was permeated to its very depths by fear of Communism and hatred of fighting, a fear and hatred which were still evident as late as 1967.

Outbreak of World War II within Greece, 1940

The Axis attack on Greece came suddenly and without warning. Shortly before dawn on October 20, 1940, Mussolini sent the Greek government an ultimatum and at the same time launched a military attack from behind the Albanian border. Greek forces were pathetically few in number and so inadequately equipped that they had to rely on ox carts to carry most of the few arms and supplies they had. General Metaxas, nevertheless, courageously decided to resist. Under the leadership of General Alexander Papagos, the Greek Chief of Staff, Greek troops held the line and even pursued the invading Italians back into Albania.

Approximately six months later, on April 6, 1941, the Germans attacked, also without warning. In less than forty-eight hours, their splendidly equipped troops and armored units had penetrated far into Greek territory, and the harbor installations in the Piraeus, the most important in the country, had been bombed into mere piles of rubbish. Almost two years previously the British had guaranteed the independence of Greece. Now, fighting on all fronts, they managed to land on Greek soil, a brief time before the Germans arrived, a small force of British, Commonwealth, and Polish troops and an almost negligible number of fighter planes. Matters went badly, and withdrawal of the forces under British command became inevitable, although many of the troops never got farther than Crete. On the way to the beaches from which the British were evacuated "the worst regret was for the unfortunate Greeks. The troops had come to feel both affection and admiration for these people who had not paused to count the cost before seeking to defend themselves with their primitive equipment against the most powerful war machine the world had ever known. . . . all the way to Athens, and on down the roads to the beaches, they [the British and other troops] met only kindness and goodwill."[1]

Removal of King George II from Athens and Formation of the Government-in-Exile, 1941

With German forces in control of the mainland, the government was removed from Athens to Crete and the King accompanied it. On the tragically beleaguered island, he revealed himself to many of his British allies as "a patriot Greek, a staunch and courageous man, undismayed by his misfortune, and already recognized by Hitler as a determined enemy."[2]

Just before troops on the island were swamped by the German tide flooding in by parachute and glider, the King was removed to Cairo and subsequently to London, which became the headquarters of the government-in-exile. This government was composed of politicians who had been out of power during the Metaxas era and who carried with them many of their old party differences. They had to face manifold difficulties in attempting to maintain any contact with the Greek people in the homeland, to control their armed forces in the Middle East, and to plan for a restoration after the end of the war.

Spread of the Occupation and Beginning of Resistance

Less than two months after the invasion the occupation covered all of Greece. The Germans themselves never occupied the whole country but permitted the Bulgarians to control eastern Macedonia and western Thrace, while the Italians were supposed to be in charge of Athens. Planning to invade North Africa, the Germans kept the lines of communication in their own hands and held the towns and cities and some of the islands, notably Crete, which was on the direct line to Africa. Soon the first of a series of puppet governments was installed within Greece, but for all practical purposes most of the mountainous countryside on the mainland was left to its own devices.

While the occupying forces were busy in the cities, bands of guerrilla fighters began to organize themselves in the remote mountains. As most of the groups were republican in sentiment, the Germans saw in them a means of strengthening opposition to the exiled Greek government under the King and so were inclined to tolerate and even encourage all of them except the Communists. The Germans also hoped that the large number of resistance groups would begin to fight among themselves, a wish destined to be fulfilled, but not until too late to aid the invading Axis forces.

Organized Resistance against the Occupation

Within less than five months after the occupation began to strangle the country the National Liberation Front (*Ethnikon Apeleftherotikon Metopon,* EAM) was created. Originally a coalition of various socialist organizations, EAM then consisted of both non-Communists and Communists, though probably more of the former. Both were attracted by the opportunity to work actively against the Germans, and few recognized that EAM was "Communist-conceived, delivered and motivated."[3] Even such a man as Elias Tsirimokos, a leader among the moderate socialists, supported the organization and stuck by it until April 1945, when its Communist control had become entirely clear to him.

It was not difficult for EAM to attract recruits for the creation of a guerrilla force, the National Popular Liberation Army (*Ethnikos Laikos Apeleftherotikos Stratos,* ELAS). Organized in April 1942 in the mountains of Macedonia and Thessaly, ELAS was the first guerrilla force to take offensive military measures against the Germans. It was the military arm of EAM, and both were controlled by Communist Party operations underground. It was impossible to separate the military from the political organization of the Communists, and it became common to speak of EAM/ELAS as one.

While the organization was particularly attractive to the young and enthusiastic because of its early daring exploits against the German invaders, many older people at first saw in it a reincarnation of the spirit of 1821. Others, regardless of political considerations, joined EAM/ELAS if it happened to be the strongest resistance group in or near their home town or mountain village. In the early stages of the resistance, EAM/ELAS built up so active an organization that "whatever may be said about the methods and directions of KKE [the Communist Party], it was largely responsible for shaking the Greek people out of the lethargy they had sunk into immediately after the occupation settled on Greece."[4] The network of EAM/ELAS was soon widespread, and many people began to realize that the organization was Communist-organized and dominated and that its ultimate aim was to take over the entire country.

Although there were numerous other resistance groups, particularly in the early days of the occupation, only one extended its influence and membership to rival the importance of EAM/ELAS. The Republican Greek Army (*Ethnikos Dimokratikos Ellinikos Stratos,* EDES) was founded by Napoleon Zervas, a former colonel in the Greek army and an ardent republican. In 1926, as a leader of the Republican armed forces, he had been involved in anti-monarchist riots in Athens. Subsequently imprisoned, he was released only after the Italians entered the country in 1940. Refused permission to rejoin the Greek army because of his earlier republican activities, Colonel (later General) Zervas established EDES in his native Epirus, and whenever possible recruited men and officers favoring the republican cause.

EAM/ELAS offered the post of Commander-in-Chief to Colonel Zervas because of his ability and republican background but, realizing the origins and control of the organization, he flatly refused. Capturing by strategem another well-known republican and man of high military reputation, Colonel Stephanos Saraphis, EAM/ELAS persuaded him to become their leader. Although he was not a Communist, he was dedicated to using any means to resist the Germans and was generally regarded as an opportunist glad to seize whatever chance might advance him personally. He was nevertheless an able general whose leadership was not the least of the reasons for the considerable success of EAM/ELAS.

Late in 1942, EAM/ELAS controlled over half the mountainous parts of the mainland where the resistance groups were in hiding, but it never succeeded in getting a real foothold in the EDES-dominated Epirus or in Crete. There the hardy mountaineers of the republican resistance, the National Organization of Crete, held the island's craggy mountain tops through the cruel German occupation. Elsewhere EAM/ELAS became so strong that "it is only fair to say that among all resistance organizations which sprang up during the year, EAM was the most successful and could truly boast of having a larger following than any others."[5]

The Allies, finally realizing the importance of Greece to their Middle East campaign, were entirely willing to use EAM/ELAS in fighting the occupation and to postpone the day of political reckoning. They found EAM/ELAS of the greatest use when it secured possession of those areas which included lines of communication between the Germans and their forces in Africa. Therefore, for a considerable period the Allies provided large amounts of equipment, munitions, and other supplies to the fighters of EAM/ELAS.

It did not take long for rivalry to develop among the various resistance groups, and particularly between EAM/ELAS and EDES. In the autumn of 1943 the situation became one of open warfare between them. At that time a large supply of arms and ammunitions was secured by EAM/ELAS as the result of their attack on the Italian Pinerolo division, which, after the capitulation of the Italians in September of that year, had volunteered to aid the Greeks against the Germans and Bulgarians. Using its new supply of weapons, EAM/ELAS attacked the EDES bands in Thessaly. This move began the long-drawn-out guerrilla warfare among the Greeks themselves and marked the first Communist attempt at possible take-over of the country by force. Soon EAM/ELAS got the upper hand, and all other resistance groups except EDES gradually disintegrated, and even it was left in control of only a small pocket of territory in Epirus.

Growth of Anti-monarchist Sentiment during World War II

Among the numerous resistance groups advocating a republic rather than return to a monarchy after the end of the war, EDES and EAM/ELAS had been the strongest. The large number of republicans who had been forced into hiding during the Metaxas era had emerged in the resistance and had added to the fires of opposition to a king, which flamed higher and higher among all the resistance groups. Many other people, including a large number of non-Communists, had similar views. Lacking communication with the homeland, the government-in-exile failed to recognize the strength of the anti-monarchist movement within Greece and the news when it reached them came as a great surprise. Most of the Greeks in exile had assumed the return of King George II to his throne to be both desirable and inevitable. He himself had promised that within six months of liberation Greece would have a fully representative government and elections for an assembly to work out a postwar constitution.

The anti-monarchist spirit also grew among the Greeks outside their country. Early in 1944 the Greek forces in the Middle East revolted against the monarchy, inspired, most people believed, by Communist organizers. Greek forces loyal to the Crown joined the British in suppressing the uprising, and it did not last long.

When the war came to an end within Greece, no resistance organization of importance in the country was willing to back the King and government-in-exile. As the Communists were growing progressively more unpopular, a so-called X group, with generally royalist sympathies, was formed in the Athens area to combat the Communists on an eye-for-an-eye and a tooth-for-a-tooth basis. Led by the flamboyant and redoubtable Cypriot-born officer of the Greek army, Colonel Georgios Grivas, the X organization carried out its aims with considerable effectiveness but eventually became interested in attacking any resistance bands, whether or not they were Communist.

The Broken Country

War and Axis occupation had left the country prostrate. In the terrible winter of 1942, less than a year after the beginning of the occupation, some 450,000 Greeks died of starvation alone. As the war years wore on, the situation became progressively worse and more deeply tragic for the people. After the withdrawal of the Germans and Bulgarians in 1944, country as well as city people were starving. The retreating armies had raided the Greek farms and had taken with them all the available livestock—sheep, goats, poultry, and cattle—and had left the country with insufficient food to feed itself. Such factories as existed were either destroyed or looted of their machinery, and the modest industrial sector

ground to a standstill. Three quarters of the large merchant
fleet lay at the bottom of the sea.

Without a Parliament or any political parties after 1936,
and with the King still in exile at the end of the war, such
governmental and administrative structure as still existed
within the country was utterly paralyzed. The government-
in-exile had been too far off and too isolated from the occupied country to follow major developments, much less details.
Many of the old party leaders had vanished, and fewer than
a handful of men emerged from the war years with any
experience or interest in running the affairs of state. The
youth of the country, long occupied in resistance fighting, had
no training for political action. They approached the problems
of politics with an individualistic bias and a guerrilla men-
tality by which small groups concentrated on fighting other
small groups.

Emergence of Two New Leaders: Georgios Papandreou and Sophoklis Venizelos

In the government-in-exile, old political differences between the Populists and the Liberals kept coming to the fore.
In 1943 they became serious enough to bring about a complete
upheaval. Then two men emerged as potential leaders from
a background of the Liberals, Georgios Papandreou, a staunch
follower of the statesman Eleutherios Venizelos, and Venizelos' son Sophoklis. Papandreou was destined to become one
of the best-known of modern Greeks.

Georgios Papandreou

Born in 1888 in Kaletzi in the Peloponnese, Georgios
Papandreou was the son of a married priest of the Orthodox

Church (clergy of the lower ranks are allowed to marry). He had studied law at the University of Athens and political science and economics at the University of Berlin. Papandreou at the age of twenty-five had already become associated with the Liberal Party of Venizelos. Soon Papandreou was appointed prefect of the city of Mytilene on the Aegean island of Lesbos. He remained an admirer and friend of Venizelos throughout the latter's life. Always influenced in his thinking by the opposition of Venizelos to King Constantine I, Papandreou resigned his post when the government of Venizelos fell in 1915 as a result of the latter's dispute with the King. Not long afterwards, Papandreou joined the group of followers of Venizelos who in 1917 carried Greece into World War I on the side of the Allies.

For the next three years Papandreou served as governor of the island of Chios. But the power of the Liberals was temporarily weakened in 1920, when Venizelos left Greece for Paris and King Constantine I returned to his throne. Papandreou found himself once more in opposition to the King and was imprisoned for four months. Elected to Parliament in 1923, he served three years; but when General Pangalos seized power in 1926, Papandreou went into exile, along with other leaders who had opposed the coup.

On his return home, after the elder Venizelos had come back to Greece from his voluntary exile in Paris, Papandreou continued to work for the Liberals. Serving in various cabinets, he was Minister of the Interior and considerably later Minister of Education and then Minister of Communications. Because of his passionate belief in the importance of education, his years in that ministry were destined to affect his future career and political program. Discontented with the speed with which social welfare was being extended throughout the neediest groups, in 1933 he set up a middle-of-the-road socialist party, the Democratic Socialist. Because neither his views nor his party were to Metaxas' liking, Papandreou was among those exiled during that period.

When he returned home again, events rapidly caught up with him, and he was imprisoned during the German occupation. Managing to escape, Papandreou reached Cairo and London, where the government-in-exile was located.

Beginnings of Postwar Government, 1944

Papandreou was not only a strong patriot and an experienced politician but also an able negotiator. In the spring of 1944, when Sophoklis Venizelos was unable to form a government lasting more than a few days, Papandreou was asked to take the helm. Deciding that the political parties alone could not do the job in a country where the dominating forces had been those of the resistance, Papandreou invited the resistance groups to be represented at a conference for the formation of a "government of national unity." The conference was held in May of that year in Lebanon because of the impossibility of summoning it in occupied Greece. The Communist-led resistance forces had been so important throughout the occupation that they were invited too. Their representatives consisted of members of the Committee of National Liberation (*Politiki Epitropi Ethnikis Apeleftheroseos,* PEEA), which had been organized in the mountain hide-outs as a kind of political adjunct to EAM/ELAS.

Withdrawal of the Axis Forces from Greece

Approximately four months after the Lebanon conference the Germans had begun to pull out of Greece, and by the end of October their withdrawal from the mainland was complete, although some forces remained in Crete and the

Dodecanese until the final German surrender in May 1945. The Germans withdrew of their own volition, because they had been cut off from exit through Yugoslavia when the Russian troops marched into that country and because they realized that if the Bulgarians deserted them in the face of the approaching Russians, there would be no possible escape northwards. "The plain fact was that Greece was liberated because the German troops left the country, and not because they were driven from it. At times the Greek guerrillas and the tiny Allied forces acting with them, had difficulty in keeping contact with the German rearguards. In Macedonia and Thrace, the position remained the same, as the Bulgarian occupying troops had changed their colors and were acting as agents of the Red Army."[7]

Papandreou's "Government of National Unity"

Returning to Athens on the heels of the German withdrawal, Papandreou set up a cabinet of his "government of national unity." Representing all the parties, it included six members of the Communist Committee of National Liberation. The government of national unity was anything but unified. It turned out to be a jangling and unruly combination in which disagreements among the old political parties at first caused more difficulties than those with the Communists. Disapproving proposed plans, however, the Communists withdrew from the government soon after its formation and remained on the outside for several months before changing their minds and deciding to take part.

The chief source of violent disagreement was the disposition of the armed forces. In September 1943 the Allies and the government-in-exile had agreed that the British Major General Scobie was to command the Allied forces, which were to land in Greece when liberation came. EAM/ELAS under Saraphis and EDES under Zervas had also consented to turn their resistance forces over to the control of the Greek government, which in turn was to place them under General Scobie. Papandreou believed that as the result of the agreement the Greek guerrilla forces would automatically come under the Scobie command. Hoping to set up a National Guard with a division of various types of resistance fighters, the Papandreou government decided to dissolve existing guerrilla organizations. Regular officers, including General Saraphis, were to be reinstated in the Greek army, although Papandreou refused to allow him to become chief of staff because of his long and important leadership in the Communist-controlled EAM/ELAS.

December Fighting in Athens and Communist Attempt to Take Over Greece by Force, 1944

As soon as the plan for dissolving the guerrilla troops was announced, and the formation of a new National Guard begun, the Communist members of the government resigned, and at Communist instigation a demonstration and general strike were called for December 2 and 3. The result, for which the Communists had hoped, was civil war, with EAM/ELAS troops fighting Greek government army and British forces in the streets of an impoverished Athens. The situation of the British troops became serious, and those in the center of the city were surrounded by EAM/ELAS forces, with only a few days' rations left. Prime Minister Winston Churchill and Field Marshal Alexander went to Greece and spent Christmas of that freezing December in Athens, trying to work out a solution for the desperate situation.[8] After taking control, they were able to rescue the British forces by sending to Athens reinforcements and supplies diverted from Italy.

Resignation of Prime Minister Papandreou, December 1944

This attempt of the Communists to win Greece by armed force was overcome, and early in 1945 EAM/ELAS gave up the struggle, at least under that name and for the time being. They had been badly mistaken in their estimate of both the Greek and British determination, strength of character, and will to resist.

Finding government impossible in the terrible struggle for Athens, Papandreou had tried to offer his resignation early in December 1944, but King George II had refused to accept it, presumably on the advice of Winston Churchill. As stated by Sir Reginald Leeper, British ambassador to the government-in-exile, Churchill "let it be known that while the British were fighting in Athens, a change of governments was undesirable."[9] So Papandreou remained as prime minister until the end of that tragic month.

Regency of Archbishop Damaskinos and Postwar
Government of General Plastiras, 1944–1945

There was general agreement that the country should have a regent until a decision could be reached concerning the return of King George II to the throne. Before leaving office, and in accordance with Greek practice of turning to the clergy for help in time of political trouble, Papandreou suggested the appointment of Archbishop Damaskinos, head of the Orthodox Church in Greece, as regent. As successor in the office of prime minister, Papandreou suggested General Nikolaos Plastiras, the well-known republican of the 1920s and 1930s and head *in absentia* of the EDES republican-dominated resistance group. He had been exiled in France for some years. The Archbishop was appointed regent at an all-party conference and took office the last day of December 1944. General Plastiras returned to Greece and entered on his duties as prime minister; he formed a caretaker cabinet on January 3, 1945.

The King had little enthusiasm for the appointment of the Archbishop and none at all for Plastiras as prime minister. The Archbishop had been removed from office under Metaxas and then restored to it by the Germans. He had refused, however, to take any part in their puppet government and after its formation was so outspoken in his criticism that he was placed under house arrest, remaining there until the country was liberated. The King objected to Damaskinos' willingness to cooperate with General Plastiras, whose republican background was obviously antipathetic to him.

That background, including republican pronouncements made during his exile in France, continued to haunt General Plastiras as prime minister. In addition to the chaotic state of the country, this handicap meant that his government was able to pull through for only three months. Because the Greeks tried to continue with their old political stage sets in the new and tragic circumstances of the years ahead, the Papandreou and Plastiras governments were the forerunners of many shifting governmental scenes to come.

Continued Attempts to Govern, 1945–1946

Without enough leaders and apparatus to govern the nation after the end of the war, Greece returned to its old political ways. The Liberals and the Populists climbed on their seesaw again and began their ups and downs as before the abolition of all parties. Slight variations in viewpoint and leadership sought expression in new parties, and the old struggle over proportional representation versus majority vote returned intensified. In the inherently chaotic situation of the last half of the 1940s, some forty or more parties are reported to have contested each other at the polls.

Governments came and went, majority governments were impossible to attain, and none of the ever-shifting coalition cabinets remained in power long enough to solve the urgent problems before the country. When no coalition was possible, and voting was carried on by proportional representation, control of Parliament went again to a small party, usually the Communist or a Communist-sponsored group. If the situation had not been so desperate and the need for reconstruction of the broken nation so great, it would have seemed that the parties were playing musical chairs, unaware that in trying to capture a place to sit they were skirting deeply serious problems to which they should have given attention.

With the era of General Metaxas receding into the background, and with the occupying Germans and Bulgarians finally gone from the country, such people as could lift their heads above their own starvation, sorrow, and tragedy wanted representative government of the country's own choosing again. They also needed to decide whether or not King George II was to return to his throne. From exile, the King made it clear that he would not go back unless he had a definite sign from the Greek people that he was wanted. Such a sign was given by a parliamentary election and then a referendum on the subject of the monarchy, following procedure established when kings had been in exile.

Greece Returns to Parliamentary Government, 1946

The elections were set for March 31, 1946, which turned out to be the same day as the Communist attack on a Thessalian village which lit the signal fires for another Communist attempt to take over Greece by force. In the fear and hatred of the early days of the guerrilla fighting, the only way to carry out an honest vote, without intimidation, appeared to be under the watchful eye of foreign observers. The Russians refused to participate and the French withdrew, but a team of American and British representatives remained in Greece to observe the procedure.

Only some 49 per cent of the electorate voted because many Greeks were still fugitives; others were afraid to vote; and the Communists refused to take part. Despite Communist statements to the contrary, Allied observers reported that politically inspired abstentions from the polls were comparatively few, constituting possibly under 10 per cent of the vote.[10]

While the mechanism for the elections was proportional representation, votes were not scattered as they usually were under that system. The Populists and the other monarchist groups secured a large majority.[11] The election, however, was not geared to give any expression of political opinion other than whether or not members to be elected to Parliament wished the King back. It became clear that he was wanted as a symbol of the prostrate nation's return to nationhood.

King George II Returns to the Throne Again from Exile, 1946

In accordance with tradition, a referendum following the election underlined the desire for King George II's return. But violent disagreement preceded the referendum as to whether it should be limited to the subject of the King's possible return to the throne or extended to the broader problem of the nation's continuation as a monarchy, no matter who the sovereign might be.

In accordance with an agreement of the Allies, their observers were given the task of supervising the compilation of the lists of eligible voters. The plebiscite, held on September 1, 1946, was limited to the single question of King George II's restoration to the throne. With 1,861,145 registered voters, 1,666,511 votes were cast in favor of the King. Despite the many accusations of dishonesty made against the voting and the count, the majority was large enough at least to indicate the temper of the Greek people. They apparently wanted King George II back as a kind of cement to hold them together in perilous times.

The returns, however, failed to indicate how many of those voting would have preferred no king at all, or how many, remembering King George's acquiescence in the dictatorial actions of Metaxas, opposed the King's return because of his action—and especially lack of action—then. Nor did the plebiscite show how many republicans chose the King's return because they feared Communism would be the alternative.

After the referendum, Archbishop Damaskinos resigned as regent and at the end of September 1946 King George II returned to the throne for the second time in his life. He was destined to remain there only a short time. Seven months after his return, just before the onset of the most violent civil strife which was to come to the storm-tossed nation, King George II died of a heart attack and was succeeded on the throne by his younger brother, Paul.

Years of Guerrilla Warfare and Communist Insurrection, 1946–1949

King Paul I began his reign in the darkest days of Communist aggression since the violent attempt at a Communist take-over of Athens in December 1944. The new onslaught began with the organization of a Communist-sponsored Democratic Army approximately a year after the end of EAM/ELAS operations in 1945. Communist attack was begun in 1946 on the political as well as the military front. On Christmas Eve, from their snow-covered mountain headquarters, the Communists announced the formation of what they called the Free Democratic Government, complete with governmental machinery of ministries and cabinet officials. Although the posts were filled with carefully chosen party members, the government turned out to be a complete fiasco; no Communist country, including the U.S.S.R., gave it even formal recognition.

Nikos Zakhariades, released from the Dachau concentration camp, had returned to Athens in May 1945, and once more had become the belligerent leader of the Greek Communist party. The death of Georgios Siantos, presumably of a heart attack in May 1947, removed the strongest advocate of political action rather than violence, and brought Zakhariades clearly to the forefront of Greek Communist decisions. Although a convinced Communist, Siantos had also been a Greek nationalist at heart. In his years in the German concentration camp Zakhariades had been removed from the currents of Communist politics as well as from Greek thought and had had no practical experience with any of the resistance organizations. He soon became personally jealous of Markos Vaphiadis, commander of the Democratic Army, and also differed with him in matters of tactics. Zakhariades advocated fighting in conventional battle formation, but the commander believed in guerrilla methods of fighting and kept his forces organized in small bands until Zakhariades insisted on change.

From 1946 to 1949, with bases and sources of supply in

Yugoslavia, Albania, and Bulgaria, the Democratic Army fought the British-organized and equipped Greek National Army and National Guard in a Communist-inspired war. In the first stages of the combat the Democratic Army was well provided with arms and munitions. Supplies and Greek guerrillas, trained in the Communist countries to the north, poured across the borders and were dropped by parachute into the Peloponnese and elsewhere in southern Greece.

So apparent did it become that much of the fighting was controlled and guided from outside the country that even today many Greeks refuse to use the term "civil war" to apply to the struggle from 1946 to 1949 and refer to it only as "Communist guerrilla war," or in Greek *andartopolemos*. It is certainly true that without the aid of the Communist countries of the north, the Democratic Army could not have come as close to victory in Greece as it did.

The Security Council of the United Nations finally intervened. During 1946 it twice refused to accept the Russian charges that the Greek government by its actions in the Balkans was disturbing international peace and security, but in November of the same year heard Greece's complaint against Albanian, Bulgarian, and Yugoslav activities on behalf of Communist guerrillas fighting in Greece. The Council appointed a United Nations Special Commission on the Balkans, on which all the members of the Security Council were represented. After a visit to Greece, the Commission reported that the Democratic Army in Greece had been receiving aid of various kinds from the three Balkan countries. The representatives of the U.S.S.R. and Poland dissented violently and called Greece itself responsible for the dispute over infiltration.

In the many divisions among the Greek Communists at the time, none loomed larger than the decision of the party in Greece to follow Stalin rather than Tito in his break with the party line of the U.S.S.R. As a result, Greek Communism received a crippling blow when Tito, expelled from the *Comintern* in 1948, decided to reduce his assistance to the Communists of Greece. With quarters, hospitals, and bases of supplies on Yugoslav territory, the Communists received the coup de grâce with the closing of the frontiers between the two countries in 1949. Albania became the chief base for Democratic Army forces, but it was not strong enough to prove a sure ally when the Democratic Army was in trouble. The U.S.S.R. failed to give aid to the Greek Communists, and finally Bulgaria was the only source of assistance left. But Bulgaria had troubles of its own, and in any case it was too late.

American Aid and Final Greek Victory

The turning of the tide came with the arrival of massive American aid for the Greek forces battling the Communists. The Greeks fought bravely in some of the most cruel fighting of modern times, but without first British and then American help they could not have succeeded in overcoming the Communists. During the early stages of the struggle the Greek National Army was given all the help a war-worn and impoverished Britain could provide, but equipment and supplies were never adequate. Another difficulty, as seen by a British authority on Communist military strategy, was the Greek army

tied down by static defense as powerful politicians used their influence to ensure that troops guarded their own local areas and they were loath to see them moved away. Accordingly GNA units could not be easily and freely switched from one place to another as required. . . . Another retarding factor was that the General Staff, under heavy political influence, was rigid and over-centralized. Division commanders could not move any of their units without its permission.[12]

After Britain was no longer able to carry the burden of aid to Greece, the United States stepped in with the Truman Doctrine in 1947, which provided a program of financial and military assistance, including equipment and training for the Greek National Army and National Guard. The appointment of General—soon to be made Field Marshal—Alexander Papagos in 1949 as Commander-in-Chief of the Greek forces meant that the command was in the hands of a man of stature, a determining factor in the final defeat of the Democratic Army that year.

Another most important factor in that defeat was the Communist inability throughout the whole period of guerrilla fighting to convince the majority of the Greeks of the value of Communism. Around them Greeks saw the horror, slaughter, and devastation which it had piled on top of the earlier destruction of war. In the last analysis there was one paramount reason for the Communist defeat. An important eyewitness in Greece during those years was Colonel C. M. Woodhouse, who was dropped into the country by parachute in 1942 and remained to become commander of the Allied Military Mission to the Greek guerrillas, and later Second Secretary of the British Embassy in Athens. According to Woodhouse, the chief reason for the Communist downfall was "the Greeks' will to survive. Alike in their resistance to the German occupation and in their refusals to submit to Communist tyranny, the spirit of the Greek people was beyond praise. There have been few more conclusive illustrations of Napoleon's dictum that in war the proportion of moral to material factors is as three to one."[13]

The tasks of reconstruction and rehabilitation were stupendous, even with large amounts of foreign aid. Some 700,000 of the peasants, a tenth of the whole population at the time, were uprooted from their blackened and destroyed villages and driven far from home where they huddled in barren refugee camps with far too little food, clothing, or heat in the cold days of winter. Thousands of city dwellers were homeless and without work, and more than 20,000 children (some estimates run as high as 28,000) had been abducted to Communist countries, although a number subsequently returned home.

The inadequate network of roads, rail transportation, and communications which had existed before the war throughout Greece had all but disappeared; practically all public services and local administrations were non-existent or badly disrupted; few schools were open for children who were too undernourished to benefit from the little education that was available. Both adults and children suffered from malaria, tuberculosis, and from malnutrition. The loss of homes, possessions, means of providing foodstuffs, and of earning a livelihood was for the starving Greeks a tragedy too great to be imagined. Only their own continuing courage and help from their allies prevented the complete collapse of the entire nation.

Attempts to Govern the Desolated Country, 1947–1949

During the years of guerrilla fighting attempts to govern Greece had to run concomitantly with the military and political struggle against the Communists. With forces invading from outside the country, with Greek fighting Greek, and with Communists sniping at all government, only a superhuman governmental structure could have survived. Returning to its prewar political party organization, and lacking strong leaders, Greece tried to govern itself from 1947 to 1949 by so-called governments of national unity to carry the nation through to a less turbulent and tragic era. Even such governments were difficult to construct and turned out to be less than unified, less than national, and far from lasting.

After Zakhariades had called for all-out war by the Communists in October 1947, and the Communist Free Democratic Government had been established, it had become abundantly clear to the Greek government that Communist political activities could no longer be tolerated. Accordingly, at the end of that year the Communist Party of Greece was banned. It immediately went underground, and many party members, including Zakhariades, fled Greece. A number of the refugees joined those who had fled earlier to Albania, Yugoslavia, and Bulgaria, while Zakhariades apparently reached the U.S.S.R.

By October 1949 chaos in Greek politics had become so great that the fleeting governments could in no way cope with the situation, and martial law was required. The nadir of shifting governments appeared to come the next month when a government was formed almost identical with the one which had preceded it, but its inner disunity was so great that the prime minister received a vote of confidence by a plurality of only one.

Elections of March 1950

After the guerrilla warfare was over, martial law was rescinded. But the ban on the Communist party remained in force, and has never been lifted.

With peace re-established, new elections were called for March 1950. All Greek men, no matter what their politics, were allowed to vote if they had taken part in the resistance against the Axis in World War II. Although the Communists were not allowed to vote under the sign of the hammer and sickle, they went to the polls without label. Instead, they became part of a coalition group, the Democratic Front or Group. Its members had widely differing viewpoints; it included non-Communists who were opposed to Greece's entry into NATO and some who were merely discontented with the *status quo*. Although the Front gained few votes, it emerged with the balance of power. It was the old story of proportional representation. Because of it, none of the parties secured a majority at the polls.[14] The Democratic Front lacked cohesiveness, various of its members refused to toe the Communist line, and it split apart after the elections.

New Center Group

The elections had important results for the future of Greek political life. The strangle hold of Populist and Liberals was broken, thanks to the emergence of a strong balancing force, the National Progressive Union of the Center (*Ethniki Proodeftiki Kentrum,* EPEK). Founded by General Plastiras, it was a moderate center group, not too unlike the Liberals, and the government later formed by it and the Liberals was responsible for Greece's acceptance of the invitation to join NATO.

CHAPTER 7

Years of Stability, 1952–1961

Instability had come to be the one stable factor in Greek political life again, and post-World War II governments came
and went one after another. Many Greeks felt the pressing
need of governmental stability, and chief among these was
Field Marshal Alexander Papagos, the outstanding personality brought forth by the war and guerrilla fighting. For driving the Italians back in 1940 and for leading the Greek
National Army to victory nine years later he had been raised
to the rank of Field Marshal and he had deservedly become
a national hero.

After the end of the guerrilla fighting in 1949, the Field
Marshal had been approached to form a government, but
he had refused, indicating he had no desire to enter any aspect
of politics. But after the 1950 elections, when he saw some
four or five governments fall in record time, his national
pride was aroused, and he was finally persuaded that by
entering the political lists he could win a degree of stability
for his country.

*Field Marshal Alexander Papagos and the Organization of
the Greek Rally, 1951*

Attempting to unite the Greeks in much the same way as
General De Gaulle did the French with *Rassemblement*

Français, Field Marshal Papagos founded the Greek Rally (*Ellinikos Synagermos,* ES) in 1951. Although he had had his own misunderstandings with the royal family, he and the Rally generally were monarchists and conservatives in sympathy, and the movement was based on many of the traditions and some of the personalities of the Populists. But the leader made a difference. In his desire for unity, he attacked the past of both Populists and Liberals as a "regime of the parties" which had failed to give Greece much-needed political and economic stability.

Appearing only five weeks before elections of September 1951, the Rally had too short a time for its campaign. Nor were there any clear-cut differences between it and its opponents of the center. The center parties were in favor of orientation toward the West and of NATO membership, as was the Rally, but the center took a more critical attitude toward the high cost of defense in the Greek budget than the Rally. The center parties were somewhat more tolerant of the Communist approach to these problems than the strongly anti-Communist Rally. Even such differences as existed between the two did not appear clearly until 1952.

Communism and Its Friends in a New Guise, 1951

In addition to the Rally, another new name appeared on the ballots, the United Democratic Left (*Enosis Dimokratiki Aristeras,* EDA). Forbidden their own clothes after 1947, the Communists reappeared in disguise, with some of the seams finished by their non-Communist friends. In most ways, however, the garment of the United Democratic Left had been tailored by the Communist Party to fit its own figure. The folds were able to hide the old-line Communists but included many non-Communists as well. The latter had joined the group as a protest against slow progress in economic rehabilitation, against Greece's pro-Western orientation, or the constantly changing positions in the country's political minuet.

In domestic affairs the United Democratic Left attracted those whose social and economic views tended to left-wing socialism if not Communism itself. In foreign affairs the United Democratic Left began its career by strong opposition to continuation of Greece's large military expenditures, which it insisted prevented a forward surge of economic development; it fought the idea of the adherence of Greece to NATO; and the party carried on propaganda for trade with eastern Europe instead of heavy concentration in the west.

Still No Clear Answer in the 1951 Elections

In an attempt to allow expression of the many shades of political opinion and especially to prevent the smaller parties from gaining more than a few seats, a voting system of modified rather than straight proportional representation was pushed through Parliament by the stronger parties. But proportional representation, no matter how modified, had always scattered the votes among a large number of small parties, and several times had thrown the control of Parliament into the hands of the Communists or Communist-controlled groups. In 1951, however, the Rally was strong enough to prevent as much scattering as might have been expected. It secured more than a third of all the votes cast and somewhat under half the seats. The National Progressive Union of the Center ran apart from the Liberals and came in second, the Liberals came in third, and the United Democratic Left trailed behind and elected only a small number of deputies.[1]

Coalition the Only Possibility for Government, 1951–1952

With election results so divided, the only possibility for a government lay in coalition. Foreseeing that any such arrangement would soon fly apart, as usually happened with coalition governments, Field Marshal Papagos refused to take part. So the National Progressive Union of the Center and the Liberals, as the two leading center parties, formed a coalition, with General Plastiras of the former as prime minister and Sophoklis Venizelos of the latter as his deputy. The coalition lived for just over a year. Gradually both the National Progressive Union and the Liberals lost supporters to the Rally, and this loss, together with the weight of the country's problems of economic rehabilitation, finally toppled the government. During its existence, the coalition tallied up a series of accomplishments which were little different from what Papagos might have done had he been at the helm, and he was in sympathy with them.

Despite their differences, Papagos and Plastiras realized that if parliamentary government were to survive, one strong party must steer the ship. Both leaders agreed that the majority system of elections was necessary to strengthen the leading parties in Parliament by concentrating the largest numbers of seats in their hands. Sophoklis Venizelos, struggling to maintain a degree of Liberal power, knew his party would secure fewer seats under the majority system and so insisted that proportional representation was the only way to provide for fair representation of all.

United States Interest in Greek Politics, 1951–1952

The situation was desperately serious. The United States was deeply involved in Greek economic reconstruction, not only from strong humanitarian motives but also to prevent a regrowth of Communism in Greece. The years 1950 and 1951 brought Greece the largest amount of aid appropriated in any one fiscal year during the entire American aid program to Greece.[2] It was clear that in the absence of political stability, the Greek nation could not rebuild its devastated economy, much less build its future. So its aid funds involved the United States in Greek politics. The American Embassy and aid missions were in strong agreement with both Plastiras and Papagos that the majority system of voting in the next elections would be the only way to produce a stable government.

As a consequence, the American officials openly advocated the single-member district arangements of the majority system. The ambassador, believing that the large sums of American aid permitted "greater American involvement in affairs which would have otherwise been considered strictly domestic"[3] issued a statement somewhat surprising in view of general practice in such matters. The ambassador indicated that "because the American government believed that the re-establishment of the 'simple proportional' method of election, with its inevitable consequences of the continuation of governmental instability, would have destructive results upon the effective utilization of American aid to Greece." The ambassador continued: "the American embassy feels itself obliged to make its support publicly known for the patriotic position of the prime minister with regard to this subject."[4] In reply, the nettled Greek government issued a statement, saying that "it belonged to the Greek people and government to decide with what election system the country will be administered."[5]

Victory of Field Marshal Papagos in the 1952 Elections

The Greeks were anxious to get ahead with the job of economic rehabilitation and development. Many were tired of the political centrifuge of proportional representation. So Field Marshal Papagos had his way; in the elections held on November 16, 1952, the majority system of voting was used. The Rally came into power on a landslide of votes, polling just less than half of all the ballots cast, and securing more than three quarters (247) of all the seats. In a Parliament with membership increased from 250 to 300, no candidate of the pro-Communist left was elected, while the Liberals and the National Progressive Union of the Center, running together, elected 51 deputies.[6] Those who were looking for stability and conservatism in government, and a close tie to the West, were able to breathe a little more freely, at least for the time being.

Field Marshal Papagos as Prime Minister, 1952–1955

As prime minister, Papagos moved ahead with much-needed economic reforms and programs of reconstruction. An economic program was announced by the young and able Spyros Markezinis, who had been made Minister of Coordination. Among its activities, this ministry oversaw and tried to coordinate the three economic ministries of the government, that is, industry, commerce, and finance, so it was the obvious organization to take charge of programs of economic development. Ever mindful of the large amount of American aid being poured into Greece, the United States Mission for Aid to Greece was not averse to taking a hand in the preparation of the program and assisting the ministries in their plans to curb inflation, to balance the budget, and to stimulate foreign investment.

The drachma was soaring in value so wildly that it caused great hardship to people whose wages and salaries were fixed. Family jewelry was sold for amounts which, though far from small, did not suffice to keep the sellers in the barest necessities of life. In January 1953 the situation was vividly illustrated to the authors when they paid several thousand drachmas for a small jar of honey.

It took political courage for the government to carry through much of its program. In 1953, with slight change the following year, the drachma was devalued and so a stable currency was achieved. At least until April 1967 it remained stable, despite economic tremors and political ups and downs. The immediate political repercussions from the financial trouble of those whose money lost its value in 1953 turned out to be less great than had been feared. In the same year the government also took the courageous step of cutting the cost of administration by releasing over 5,000 civil servants, most of whom had been engaged in the days of the Communist insurrection, when almost no paid employment was available to the white-collar class, many of whom were literally starving. Through these strong moves of devaluation and reduction of government costs, the Papagos government caused temporary difficulties but eventually improved its own balance and standing.

Under the prime minister's leadership Greece's international relations in many ways improved. Remaining firmly anti-Communist and pro-Western, the Greek government entered an agreement with the United States allowing the use of certain Greek territory by American armed forces. Greece had become a far from negligible member of the Western alliance. By 1955, nevertheless, Greek relations with the Communist countries to the north had begun to improve. Trade agreements were entered with several eastern European nations, and by an official visit to Greece President Tito of Yugoslavia gave a sign of renewed good relations between the two countries. Some of the children who had been taken from Greece during the guerrilla fighting were sent home. But the otherwise bright international picture was seriously marred by the bitterness between Greece and Britain, and later between Greece and Turkey, over Cyprus. The chasm widened, and in 1954 Prime Minister Papagos requested that the United Nations Assembly take up the matter.

Within Greece the forces for stability in economic and political affairs had not yet become firmly rooted. During the long illness of Papagos before his death in October 1955, voices were raised over his failing abilities to carry the burden, and especially over the unpopular aspects of his government's economic and international programs. For example, Spyros Markezinis, Minister of Coordination, resigned in 1954 over economic differences.

On the international front discussions centered around the Greek-American agreement for military bases in Greece. All the opposition parties insisted that the agreement had been adopted and ratified illegally as Parliament was not in session and the King was away when the action was taken by the Prime Minister and his government. The center parties, with small differences between them, disapproved of the terms of the agreement, while the United Democratic Left urged the abandonment of the Western alliance and an ultimate orientation toward eastern Europe.

Most Greeks, however, did not agree with the United Democratic Left viewpoint. One scholar of Greek foreign policy indicated that "at least 80 per cent of the Greeks endorsed a Western orientation. . . . This was based on not only cultural affinities but also geopolitical imperatives and economic and military considerations. Non-communist Greece felt itself threatened by Communist neighbors."[7]

A New Political Figure, Constantine Karamanlis, Appointed Prime Minister, 1955

After Prime Minister Papagos' death, one of the Rally's heretofore less prominent members, Constantine Karamanlis, was appointed prime minister by the King. It was a surprising choice, for it failed to follow the general practice by which the king chooses the next in command of the Rally, in this case the Deputy Prime Minister, Panayotis Kanellopoulos. Yet the little-recognized Karamanlis was to be so strong a prime minister that he was able to guide his country's fortunes uninterruptedly from 1955 until 1963, a record length of time in Greek politics.

Born in 1907 in a small Macedonian village when the Turks were still in control of the area, Constantine Karamanlis was the first Greek from Macedonia ever to attain the office of prime minister. His father, who, as sometimes happens in Greek villages, combined the vocations of farmer and teacher, died when his eldest son was still young. Constantine then became head of the family, responsible for his seven brothers and sisters. This was no small matter considering the Greek custom that demands the marriage with prearranged dowry of all the girls in the family before the brothers can marry and establish themselves. Young Constantine nevertheless managed to get to Athens, where he studied law. He later went back to practice in the town of Serres, not far from where he was born.

Elected to Parliament when he was twenty-eight, Karamanlis was re-elected many times, though he had to absent himself from all political activity during the years of Metaxas and wartime occupation. After World War II Karamanlis served in various ministries in different cabinets—labor, transport, social welfare, communications, defense, and public works. The last post brought him into prominence because of his activities in the reconstruction of Athens. Then King Paul I, seeing in the 45-year-old Karamanlis a man of the ability and determination of which Greece was so in need, appointed him prime minister.

Karamanlis and His Party of the National Radicals

Even so staunch a follower of Papagos as Karamanlis was both unable and unwilling to hold the Rally together. Like other Greek political parties, it had been based primarily on the personality of its leader, whose death, as Karamanlis said, "it was unable to survive." So the new leader resorted to the time-honored device of taking over much of the organization, membership, and policies of the old party. The new National Radical Union (*Ethniki Rizopastiti Enosis,* ERE) inherited the generally conservative mantles of both the Populists and the Rally. But in the eyes of many people it had a somewhat more progressive outlook in economic matters as well as a different name. When invited by the Populists to join with them in the pre-election campaign, the Union rejected the offer and turned to the Liberals instead.

Karamanlis Comes into Power in the 1956 Elections

The King issued a decree dissolving Parliament in the January following Papagos' death, and elections were held within the month. To fight what already appeared to be a strong new organization, a number of other parties decided to join in a pre-election group. All the small parties which had inherited the Liberal traditions of the elder Venizelos were included; at the other extreme were the Populists, generally conservative, who, like the Liberals, were fighting a losing battle to keep their strength and identity; between the two was the National Progressive Union of the Center, which had already lost a number of its followers to the Rally; and the Democratic Party founded by Papandreou, a small middle-of-the-road group interested primarily in the promotion of social welfare. Fearing that they could not make the grade alone, the motley collection, after considerable soul searching, decided to cooperate for purposes of the election with the Communist-oriented United Democratic Left. The group called themselves the Democratic Union and adopted domestic and foreign platforms which were vague, general, and subject to enough interpretations to satisfy most of their members. Although the Communist-dominated United Democratic Left influenced their outlook, they in turn exercised so much influence on it that, at least for the period of the campaign and the elections, it adopted a more moderate and less anti-Western tone than usual.

With so many groups, the Democratic Union could hardly fail to win a considerable portion of the vote in the 1956 elections. As expected, it emerged from them with a slightly larger vote than the new National Radical Union of Karamanlis, but with a small number of deputies.[8] The reason lay in the complicated arrangements for voting, in which the majority system was used in some electoral districts, proportional representation in others, and a mixed system in still others. It was an apparent attempt to be all things to all men but did actually favor the National Radicals. As matters turned out, the vote of the United Democratic Left was so small that their contribution to the total of the Democratic

Union votes was minimal. But the Left believed inclusion with the Liberals and Populists gave them an aura of respectability. A completely disparate group of parties, united in nothing save opposition to the National Radicals, the Democratic Union made no effort to solidify itself after the election but broke up almost immediately once Parliament had begun its new session.

The Karamanlis Government at the Helm, 1956–1958

In its first two years in office the Karamanlis government was unable to accomplish enough to make the success of its program of economic development either clear or sure, and it certainly was not spectacular enough to appeal widely to the economically or politically discontented. In foreign affairs the picture was blackened by the ever-heavier cloud of Cyprus. In the March following the 1956 elections, Archbishop Makarios of Cyprus was arrested and exiled by the British, and as a result the Greek ambassador was recalled from Britain. While trying to avoid an anti-British stand and sticking to the Western alliance generally, Karamanlis also supported the Greek Cypriots. He refused to agree to a policy of political neutrality which was being urged on him. On the other hand, he reached trade agreements with the U.S.S.R., Poland, and Japan, and the ban on trade with Communist China—originally imposed to please the Americans—was removed. In practice, of course, the abolition had little effect because of the small amount of Greece's trade with China.

After discussion at a NATO Conference in December 1957, the question of possible installation on Greek soil of nuclear missile bases assumed paramount importance. The National Radical government insisted on postponing a decision *pro* or *con* until the missiles were actually made available. The center parties, however, thus far pro-United States and pro-NATO, underwent considerable reversal of their stand by opposing installation. The United Democratic Left, as might have been expected, continued to push for separation from NATO and for a neutralist program which nevertheless would continue to be friendly with the United States.

The waters were still deeply troubled by disillusionment over Cyprus and the issue of Greece's Western orientation. Karamanlis lost some of his support in Parliament, including two of his ministers, over his handling of the Cyprus issue and the rumors of the establishment of nuclear bases within Greece. But the fall of his government in the winter of 1958, was precipitated, although not caused, by dispute over the method of conducting the elections ahead.

Another Karamanlis Victory in 1958

When the elections were held in May of that year the number of parties and groups which presented themselves at the polls was confusing, but at least they showed various gradations of opinion concerning issues as well as personalities.[9] The National Radicals and Karamanlis, however, were firmly entrenched in public opinion, and they emerged as victors, gaining a majority over all their combined opponents.[10] To the surprise of many the United Democratic Left, having found the time propitious, had run the race without companions and came in second. Usually 12 to 15 per cent of the vote had gone to the United Democratic Left, but in these elections it tallied up just under a quarter of the total. This represented a 15 per cent increase in votes from the preceding election, and that in turn netted a gain in deputies amounting to 300 per cent. The United Democratic Left thus achieved greater gains in Parliament than in actual number of votes.

Among the reasons for the sudden rise were the voting arrangements. Under a system of reinforced proportional representation, added seats were given to the party or coalition of parties winning the second largest part of the total vote above a certain percentage. The complicated system had been adopted under pressure by the center parties in an effort to improve their chances of securing larger representation. But it failed of its purpose.

Circumstances favored the Left at the polls. Economic progress had not been fast enough to suit a number of the disadvantaged or the disaffected protesters of things as they were. In international affairs the United Democratic Left profited by the lack of progress toward *énosis* of Cyprus with Greece, and by the rumors that the United States favored Turkey in the dispute, and that American nuclear missile bases were about to be placed on Greek soil.

Difficulties of Karamanlis and the National Radicals, 1958–1960

Gradually the domestic policies of Prime Minister Karamanlis began to show positive and recognizable effects on the economy. The wheels of industry moved more rapidly; exports showed a slight increase; the tourist industry shot ahead as Greece became known as a sun-drenched haven for travelers from Europe and America. With fiscal stability, Greeks began to deposit money in Greek savings accounts instead of buying gold sovereigns, such as had long been the habit in time of crisis, or land and luxury-type apartment houses. There was improvement in both Greek and foreign industrial investment.

There were, however, deep-seated difficulties in the economy, and it was easy to make the Prime Minister the scapegoat. As the second largest group in Parliament, the United Democratic Left became the spokesman for the opposition parties and exploited the country's readily dramatized problems to the full. On the home front there were still many poor, much unemployment and underemployment, and the gap between the city and country people's income was increasing. While the farmer's earnings were rising, the city worker's income was rising faster. The large-scale exodus from the countryside and from Greece itself in search of higher wages in countries of Western Europe, especially West Germany, was blamed on the National Radicals. Their difficulties on the home front were compounded when in 1959 and 1960 various suspected Communists were put on trial for subversive activity.

In foreign affairs the United Democratic Left, although not always opposing the presence of Greece in NATO, dwelt on the possibility of limiting its participation as much as possible. Signature by the Karamanlis government of the London and Zürich agreements with Turkey giving Cyprus independence had little appeal within Greece, and those opposed to the government found the failure to secure *énosis* an easy point on which to condemn the National Radicals.

Old Faces in New Guises; the Birth of the Center Union, 1960

Many of Karamanlis' opponents, and even some of those who had been his supporters, were tired of having one party in power for so long. Not least in importance among those against him and his party were the politicians who had been on the outside since 1955 and even since 1952 and were anxious for a share again in the political spoils so long denied them. Some of the opponents, in the Center as well as the Left, objected to the government's constant emphasis on economic development and financial stability rather than on social welfare as the country's primary goal. Some thought of Karamanlis and his followers as too strongly royalist. Others besides those oriented toward the United Democratic Left disliked the National Radical foreign policy and what they deemed its slavish following of the United States. They were anxious for Greece to build up its trade and governmental contacts with the nations of eastern Europe.

The many shades of economic and political interest were represented, as always, by a large number of parties differing from each other chiefly in personalities and only slightly in opinion. Altogether some nine parties clustered around the center in 1960, but their one unifying desire was to break the power of the Prime Minister and the National Radicals.[11] So they swallowed their disagreements long enough to form a new party, the Center Union (*Énosis Kentron,* EK). The organization included individuals as well as groups of widely divergent political and economic viewpoints and of differing ambitions and hopes. As a result, the Center Union turned out to be more of a combination of factions trying to gain power and less of a politically effective unified party with a coherent program.

The leading architects of the Center Union were Georgios Papandreou and Sophoklis Venizelos, the two long-time Liberals who had meanwhile come to head two different parties. Venizelos was the chief of what was left of the old Liberal Party founded by his father, while Papandreou still headed his own party. Associated with, but not of the group, was the Progressive Party (*Komma Proodetikon,* KP) of Spyros

Markezinis, a somewhat Right-of-Center party particularly dependent upon its leader for orientation and direction. Papandreou, as the more persuasive personality, became chief of the new group. After serving as prime minister of the difficult postwar government in 1944, he had continued in and on the fringes of politics. He had long been a deputy in Parliament. He had agreed to take part in several governments during the latter part of the 1940s, but they had never succeeded in gaining power. In 1952 his election to Parliament had been on the ticket of the Greek Rally. He realized it was the only party at the time which could give Greece the necessary stable government, and he knew that being on this ticket was the only practical way in which he could succeed in being a part of the government.

Position of the Communist-Dominated Left in 1961

For the elections of 1961, the United Democratic Left sought to join the Center Union in a pre-election agreement, but their differences were too deep-seated. The two Leftist parties, joining only with a minor Communist-oriented farm group, faced the elections and those to come under the name of the Pan-Democratic Agrarian Front of Greece. They campaigned against all aspects of the policy of the National Radicals, particularly on foreign affairs, and again accused them and the Center Union of blindly following the lead of the United States.

Karamanlis and the National Radicals Win a Resounding Victory, 1961

In the years since 1956, when Karamanlis and the National Radicals had come into power, enough time had passed for the *outs* to think that they might become the *ins* at the next election. But their hopes were doomed to disappointment.

Karamanlis and the National Radicals felt sure enough of themselves and their large majority to be willing to test their popularity at the polls, and so elections were held at the end of October 1961. Their faith had not been misplaced. Securing a fraction of a per cent less than half of all the votes, and 174 seats in Parliament, the National Radicals won the greatest electoral victory since that of Papagos and the Greek Rally in 1952. The Center Union and its small temporary ally, the Progressive Party of Markezinis, secured somewhat over a third of the votes and a third of all the seats in Parliament, while the United Democratic Left, under its new name, lost ground. It won only two-thirds of the votes and considerably under a third of the seats it had obtained in its brief hour of pride in 1958.[12]

The reasons for the United Democratic Left's decline that year were not far to seek. The election was fought primarily on the domestic front, and there was much evidence that the phoenix-like Greek economy was rising from its ashes. In foreign affairs, the missile scare had lessened, the old rug of military expenditures had been worn thin from repeated beatings, and the situation of Cyprus, although still disturbingly serious, was no longer so great an emotional red flag as to serve as a rallying point. The only new issue had been Greece's recently acquired association with the Common Market.

The few basic differences between the policies of the Center Union and those of the National Radicals clustered around the ways of fulfilling the need for more attention to "the common people" of Greece. Lacking concrete differences, the Center Union looked for reasons to disagree. They found one immediately after the elections. So great had been the margin of victory of the National Radicals that it was easy to suspect dishonesty. Assisted by the unsolicited, and undesired, support of the United Democratic Left, the opposition to the National Radicals gathered and complained loudly of fraud and intimidation at the polls. The accusation was not new in Greek politics, nor indeed was the actuality. The method of attack on it was new. The Center Union and the United Democratic Left shook the issue as a dog shakes a bone and finally used it for their main weapon against the National Radicals as a party and against Karamanlis personally.

Within a year Papandreou, leading one faction and Venizelos, leading another, had begun the attack on the National Radicals on other grounds. They reiterated the by now familiar complaints against Greece's expenditures for military purposes. But Papandreou proposed a contribution for defense to be made by each member of NATO in accordance with its economic assets and liabilities. The Center Union also raised a serious charge—that the National Radicals had infiltrated not only the civil service but even the armed forces.[13] The military was apparently still involved in politics and destined to play a far greater role on the political stage ahead.

Rumblings of Discontent with the Monarchy

To most Greeks, except those of the far Left or of the strongest republican beliefs, the institution of the monarchy appeared as the one continuing stable factor in the nation. Many realized that even under the stability brought by Papagos and Karamanlis currents of instability swirled, and these people believed that only the existence of the monarchy kept these currents from overflowing.

King Paul I was a man of poise and calm, and he typified the stability Greece needed. To the doctrinaire republicans and the pro-Communist Left, however, no king, no matter how good or how wise and poised, could ever be satisfactory. At the other extreme were those in whose eyes a king could do no wrong and who refused to admit that there was anyone in Greece except the Communists who did not want a king. Between the two extremes were many who wanted a monarch but differed among themselves as to what his constitutional powers were or should be.

A number of people who were not members of the political opposition, whether of the Center Union or the far political Left, objected to the cost of maintaining a royal family in a nation as poor as Greece. In 1964 the king received an annual allowance of $566,000, of which $313,000 went for state journeys, palace maintenance, entertainment, and wages for the palace staff. Those who opposed expenditures for royalty criticized the large dowry provided in 1962 to Princess Sophia, eldest daughter of King Paul and Queen Frederika, as they did the expense of the princess's elaborate wedding which followed. The opposition in Parliament, including both anti-Communists and pro-Communists, voted against the expenditure. At about the same time the Queen's Fund, a charitable organization, came under harsh but vague attack because it was not required to account publicly for its income and expenditures. Other opponents of the royal family, looking back to the family's Danish origins, also bore in mind that Queen Frederika, mother of Crown Prince Constantine, was German by origin. Many regarded her as too influential in crown matters and feared her influence over her son. At the very least, she was a strong, intelligent, and dominating woman, clinging to much in her German background that seemed to many Greeks strongly dictatorial.

In 1962 and 1963 the royal family and one of its journeys suddenly came into the political limelight.

Sudden Resignation of Prime Minister Karamanlis, 1963

Impatient after so long an absence from any share in political control, the opposition groups in Parliament waged an increasingly vindictive campaign, accompanied by steadily louder murmurs of fairly widespread discontent with the economic as well as the political situation. Progress on the domestic front was unsatisfactory to many, and there were fears of riots and other civil disturbance if a way out were not found. The opposition to the National Radicals attempted to persuade King Paul to invoke his constitutional power to dissolve Parliament and call new elections because, they said, the political interests of the people had not been properly represented in a Parliament chosen in the 1961 elections by fraud and dishonesty. When the King refused to accede to the request, Papandreou, as the leader of the opposition parties, accused the King of favoring the National Radicals and of establishing himself as leader of the ultra-conservatives. King Paul inadvertently added to the campaign by saying to a group of officers of the armed forces that he belonged to them and they belonged to him. The opposition played on this as an indication that the military were serving the cause of the monarchy rather than the country at large. Papandreou issued a statement warning the King against pursuing "a personal policy" as his father had.[14] About the same time a newspaper opposing the National Radicals published the old story of the feud between King Constantine I and the elder Venizelos.

The political atmosphere was altogether uneasy in 1962 and 1963. Beneath the surface, disagreements between the

Prime Minister and the royal family appeared to be growing. The Prime Minister evidently was unhappy over the Queen's activities, including her interference in political matters. But it was a minor dispute rather than a major issue between the King and the royal family which precipitated Prime Minister Karamanlis' sudden resignation in June 1963.

The preceding April, Queen Frederika had gone to London, where she was greeted by demonstrations demanding the release of Antony Ambatielos, a Communist serving a life sentence in Greece for sedition. His wife, living in London, created considerable disturbance when she tried to force her way to Queen Frederika with a petition. Soon thereafter the King and Queen proposed a state visit to England for July. The Prime Minister unsuccessfully tried to dissuade them from going. The opposition parties in Parliament took no stand on the matter, so their opinions were not apparent.

Karamanlis was strongly in favor of the monarchy, but he was tired of his various disputes with the royal family. It was rumored that the King too was weary of disagreements. The issue which prompted the Prime Minister's resignation was not an important one; it was an unfortunate choice of Karamanlis' to stand up to the royal family. The whole affair did provide a non-political reason to break the royal tie with the Prime Minister. In the light of events to come, the disagreement was a tragic one. It had the unfortunate effect of precipitating the resignation from office and self-imposed exile from Greece of one of its ablest men.

CHAPTER 8

From Right to Center
and the New Left, 1963–1965

After his resignation as prime minister in the early summer of 1963, Karamanlis went to Switzerland, evidently thinking that he would win without difficulty the elections scheduled for the following November. Absent from Greece from June until just before the elections, he failed to assess the political climate correctly. He knew he had many loyal supporters, and the stability of government and the clear economic advance under his guidance had brought him a large following. Because his resignation was precipitated by differences with the King, Karamanlis found himself with some unsolicited anti-monarchist support. But he failed to realize that in Greece, as in other countries, people tire of having one party in power for a long time. Nor had he understood the extent of his political liabilities.

Campaign against Karamanlis and the National Radicals, 1963

These weaknesses were exploited to the full in the campaign against Karamanlis by the Center Union. This party depended heavily on its leader, Georgios Papandreou, whose oratorical and maneuvering skill were of the greatest use to the party's campaign. Within the Center Union, however, there were more discordant than unifying elements. The chief figures in the party, notably Papandreou and Venizelos, spent much time struggling with each other for leadership. Eventually they found it impossible to work as a team, and only the death of Venizelos after the 1963 elections was to bring the struggle to an end. There were other strongly divergent personalities: for instance, the able, conservative, and opportunistic banker; Constantine Mitsotakis, and Elias Tsirimokos, a socialist leader well remembered for his resistance activities during World War II.

The many opposing elements of the Center Union found it difficult to agree on a program, and the party's appeal remained essentially negative. What Papandreou referred to as "the relentless struggle" was more of a fight to "get the rascals out" than to present a coherent program differing in fundamentals from that of the National Radicals.

Papandreou and his followers realized that in a world of rising expectations the Greeks could not be expected indefinitely to sacrifice social gains for the long-range goals of industrialization and economic development to which the National Radicals had devoted their chief efforts. In addition, competition ahead in the Common Market appeared too remote for most people to sacrifice immediate rewards and fail to fulfill pressing needs. Popular desire, for instance, for the greater extension of educational facilities than the National Radicals had thought the country could afford caused riots and strikes in December 1962. There was continued pressure thereafter until the National Radicals satisfied some of the more urgent educational demands.

The Center Union, seconded by the United Democratic Left, called attention to what they considered the large gaps in the whole Karamanlis program for economic and social

development. Still dwelling on their charges of dishonesty
by the National Radicals in the 1961 elections, the Center
Union promised honesty and freedom from corruption. Together with the United Democratic Left, they underlined the
charge heavily that under Karamanlis Greece had become a
police state through interference with freedom of the press,
holding of prisoners from the years of guerrilla warfare, and
bringing new trials for subversion. The National Radicals
replied that only those were still detained who had been
imprisoned after conviction in court of definite and proven
charges of murder or other serious crimes, whether committed
during the years of guerrilla fighting or later. All those found
eligible were being released, and others still in exile were
being allowed to return to Greece after proper checking and
examination.[1] But the situation became grist for the mills of
the Center Union and of the United Democratic Left. The
anti-government and anti-Karamanlis campaign grew more
and more vociferous, even extending abroad. Karamanlis
began to be called, with increasing vehemence, a "fascist"
and a "traitor."

The general promises and the never-ending campaign of
vilification began to pay off for the Center Union and to a
much smaller extent for the United Democratic Left. Combined with the desire of the voters for a change, the campaign
sapped National Radical strength and provided another reason why Karamanlis, reputedly intolerant of criticism, took
his time about returning home before the elections.

Defeat of Karamanlis and the National Radicals in the Elections of 1963

As the elections approached, the number of parties contesting at the polls had narrowed down to three, and that very

fact seemed to bode a clearer choice for the voters. The chief contestants were the National Radicals and the Center Union —the latter supported by the tiny and exceedingly personal Progressive Party of Markezinis. The only other party of importance in the race was the United Democratic Left, no longer tied to the Greek Agrarian Movement which had failed to give the support they needed.

The bitterness of the two other leading contestants against the National Radicals became steadily more apparent as the machinery for elections was being set up. As a routine matter, a king always appointed a new prime minister as head of a caretaker, non-political government to take charge of every election. In 1963 King Paul chose for the task Panayotis Pipinelis, his own former constitutional adviser, and more recently Minister of Trade and Commerce in the National Radical cabinet. Harping on the theme of the dishonesty in the 1961 elections, as they had for the past two years, the opposition parties refused to give him a vote of confidence even for a caretaker post. Parliament was composed of such a high proportion of National Radicals that Pipinelis never-theless received his vote, despite abstention of the members of the Center Union and the United Democratic Left. Both these parties insisted they would trust no one from the Na-tional Radicals to see that the elections would be carried on honestly and fairly and threatened to boycott them if held under Pipinelis' auspices. Finally Pipinelis resigned and the King then chose a man not involved in politics, Stylianos Mavromihalis, President of the Areopagos or Supreme Court, and so secured approval by both the Center Union and the National Radicals. With their vote of confidence, he was able to take charge of the elections scheduled for November 3.

The outcome of the elections might easily have been fore-told. As far as political parties and the machinery of elections went, the more the situation had changed, the more it re-mained the same. Even with a limited number of parties contesting, the country found itself with the same results at the polls that it had come to know so well. Carried out by some form of proportional representation as had been used in all elections since 1958, these elections put the Communist-dominated United Democratic Left once more in the driver's seat by giving it the balance of parliamentary power. The Center Union polled a higher proportion of the total vote than the National Radicals and so secured a few more dep-uties, but the two major contestants were too closely balanced[2] for either one to secure control of the situation. Proportional representation was again a culprit but not the only one. Individualism and the cult of personalities were still basic to the difficulties, and the struggle was in considerable measure a personal one between Papandreou and Karamanlis.

There was one hopeful sign, however. The elections showed that the campaign for honesty at the polls and in the count of votes had paid off. Competent observers believed that "the elections held on 3 November 1963 may well go down in history as the most impartial and honest elections ever conducted in Greece, where localized intimidation and minor fraud had been the rule in elections ever since the country acquired its independence."[3]

Karamanlis Leaves Greece, 1963

The defeat of the National Radicals and the campaign against him personally left Karamanlis so embittered that he resigned as party chief, departed from Greece a month after the elections, and was still living in Paris when the coup d'état came in April 1967. His successor as head of the party was his uncle-in-law, Panayotis Kanellopoulos, who had been asked by King Paul to form a government in June 1963 when Karamanlis resigned as prime minister; but Kanellopoulos had been unable to muster enough support. Kanellopoulos was an experienced, conservative, and courageous politician who had been one of the first to escape from the German occupation in World War II and reach the government-in-exile with news of what was happening within Greece.

Record of Karamanlis as Prime Minister, 1955–1963

During the eight years in which Constantine Karamanlis was prime minister there was no doubt that the nation had been set on a clear path of economic development. The wounds of the war and the years of fighting after it had been almost healed and Greece had become a developing country on the economic front. The program initiated by Prime Minister Papagos had been carried on and amplified especially in policies which maintained the stability of the drachma, held the line on prices and wages, and tried to attract foreign investment.

By establishing industrialization as its chief objective, the Karamanlis government took a great step toward bringing the country into line with the industrialized nations of western Europe. By offering various incentives for domestic and foreign participation in Greek enterprises, the National Radicals' program made every effort to enlarge and improve the industrial base of Greece. Only moderate success attended the efforts to attract Greek investment because of the continuing reluctance of most Greeks to invest in anything but family enterprises. The law enacted under National Radical sponsorship for the protection of foreign investment, however, attracted a number of new ventures, including the $200 million Esso-Pappas oil refinery and petrochemical complex in Thessaloniki, which began operations in 1966. Only slightly less important was the $125 million Aluminium de Grèce, formed to exploit Greece's most important mineral deposit, bauxite, the ore from which aluminum is derived. Also completed in 1966, the plant exports raw and refined ores, as well as the metal itself.

Although not without pressure from the Center Union, the National Radicals had the vision and courage to associate Greece with the Common Market as of July 1961 in a move which would ultimately bring the country into competition on an equal basis with the nations of western Europe. The step of association with the Market, while showing that Greece was on the way to an industrial coming of age, nevertheless meant that the country would have to improve its industrial and agricultural productivity rapidly to meet the competition ahead.

The Karamanlis government failed to change Greece's basic agricultural dilemmas. Subsidies on wheat, tobacco, and other traditional crops served to increase farm incomes but to continue the old problems. The government seemed politically fearful of taking the Draconian measures that were necessary to speed the needed changes from existing crops to those needed in a more modern economy.

Economic development costs money and the large Greek expenditures for defense cost much more. Much political capital was made over the large military expenditures. As early as 1959 the growing excess of imports over exports had repercussions in the balance of payments. Although not lacking interest in the promotion of educational and welfare services, the National Radical government was reluctant to increase their budgets as much as some might have wished because it could not afford both such services and large-scale development programs and military expenditures. The government displeased many who did not want to wait for more, and better, educational and social services, but what it lost politically from them it recouped from others. Tightening the government belt meant that the budgetary situation was improved, and this in turn bred confidence in the strength of the economy and in the government itself.

The economic strength of Greece was reinforced by the devotion to the Western Alliance always shown by the Karamanlis government. It helped stabilize the Greek position at home, in the West, and in the United Nations as well. Throughout the National Radicals' years of control, Greece's disillusionment continued to grow over the lack of progress towards *énosis* for the Cypriots with Greece. The government, however, never shifted its allegiance to NATO and the West; it merely became more insistent in its defense of the Greek viewpoint toward Cyprus.

Most vehemently pursued of the negative charges against the Karamanlis government remained the long terms of those still in prison from the days of war and guerrilla fighting. When the government instituted new trials for subversion in 1959 and 1960 many freedom-loving Greeks who were neither Communists nor Communist sympathizers were deeply perturbed, and the Communists played on their feelings.

Papandreou's Choice, 1963

Most potent among the reasons why the Center Union came out ahead of the National Radicals in the 1963 elections was the desire of the people for change and the exploitation of the Center Union by the skillful politics of Papandreou. With only 138 Center Union deputies as against 132 for the National Radicals, the Center Union had to move cautiously.

In accordance with tradition, the King appointed the chief of the largest party in Parliament prime minister, and so Papandreou was selected for the office. After his appointment, Papandreou had two choices, neither one happy: a coalition or a minority government. Unwilling to work in a coalition with such bitter opponents as the National Radicals or with those with whom he disagreed so completely as the United Democratic Left, Papandreou decided to try a minority government and so immediately set up a Center Union cabinet.

On Christmas Eve, 1963, just as the Cyprus fires burst into flame, the new government of Greece secured a vote of confidence, but only because it accepted the 28 votes which the United Democratic Left was willing to give. Papandreou, however, had found the Communists to be impossible bedfellows in 1944, and he was unwilling to give his party the taint of cooperating with them. Feeling sure that if new elections were held the Center Union would win greater support, he chose to resign immediately and call new elections.

Clear Victory and Large Majority for Papandreou, 1964

After Papandreou resigned, the King asked Panayotis Kanellopoulos as leader of the National Radical Party to form a government. He was unable to set up a coalition because of Papandreou's still adamant refusal to cooperate with him and his minority party. So Parliament was dissolved, and Ioannis Paraskevopoulos, deputy governor of the National Bank of Greece and a man outside the stream of party politics, was able to form a non-political government to oversee the elections.

Papandreou used the interval after the end of his brief term as prime minister to solidify his position within the

Center Union and to campaign for the elections. Although vaguely stated, his program promised that the debts of the farmers to the state would be adjusted, taxes reduced, tax delinquents—of whom there were many—made to pay what they owed, and, above all, education would be modernized, improved in quality, and extended in scope. These promises Papandreou and the Center Union set about fulfilling once they were elected to office. Meanwhile the Papandreou campaign had endeared the Center Union leader to the poor voters and made him unpopular with many of the rich. His spellbinding oratory and his press support had great appeal for masses of the voters, whether they heard him in person or over the radio, or even read what he said. Other people who did not like his method of presentation called him a demagogue.

The government, making ready for the 1964 elections, was able to keep Cyprus from assuming an important part in the campaign, and the two major political parties agreed not to use it as an issue. Neither they nor any other political group, including even the pro-Communist Left, raised any objection to the monarchy as an institution or to the King as an individual, and so neither was an issue in the election campaign.

The system of voting became a serious difference between the Center Union and the National Radicals in the days preceding the elections and again showed the shifting nature of Greek political premises. When they controlled the situation the National Radicals had chosen either reinforced proportional representation or a combination of it and the single-member district voting. Now that their grasp had slipped, they advocated simple proportional representation as the best means of lessening the number of parliamentary seats of the Center Union and assuring some for themselves.

When the elections came on February 14, 1964, it was clear that the people were completely ready for a change. As in 1963, not even a whisper was heard that the elections were not honestly and fairly conducted, and in none of the electoral districts were there any contested ballots. With 53 per cent of the total vote, the largest ever secured by any one party, the Center Union with 173 deputies had a clear majority. The National Radicals (this time supported by the Progressives who had deserted their backing of the Center Union) secured slightly more than a third of the total vote and 105 seats, and the United Democratic Left lost a small percentage of its former vote and emerged with 22 deputies.[4]

The reason for the drop in the Communist-controlled vote came in considerable part from a change in their tactics. Realizing that in some areas they had so little strength that they had no chance of winning, the United Democratic Left did not put up any candidates in just under half of the electoral districts. It preferred to gain influence by infiltrating other parties, notably the Center Union. In many places, therefore, a voter who wished to bet on a winning candidate had no practical choice other than between the Center Union and the National Radicals. The vote of the United Democratic Left was thus hidden in the returns of the Center Union.

In the 1964 elections one party, the Center Union, clearly emerged as victor at the polls with a large majority, and so secured the mandate to go ahead with its program. Even those who were not especially favorable to the Center Union's politics and program breathed a sigh of relief. The eight months of uncertainty after the resignation of Karamanlis was over. Although there were some signs of economic disquiet, it looked as though Greece could move further along the road to economic development while continuing the political stability of the years since 1952. Other nations of western

Europe with a large number of parties, no one of which ever clearly won the race, looked enviously at Greece.

King Constantine II Succeeds to the Throne, 1964

King Paul, dying of cancer in 1963 and 1964, lived just long enough to swear in the Papandreou government. It was assumed that young King Constantine II, the second child and only son of King Paul and Queen Frederika, would have as auspicious a reign as his father's had turned out to be. But the political stability which many people believed to be firmly rooted proved a will-o'-the-wisp. The new King's rule was destined to be full of storm and stress, at least in its early years.

Constantine was born in 1940 and soon thereafter was baptized at a service in which, prophetically enough, the Greek armed forces were among his godparents. In early childhood training for his future responsibilities began, and he attended his father's audiences with members of the cabinet and accompanied him on various missions. At the age of sixteen the Crown Prince was given honorary military rank and on coming of age was made an officer of the three armed services.

Ascending the throne when he was twenty-four, the young king was married in 1964 to a distantly related Danish royal princess, Anne-Marie. Emotional royalists glowed with pride over the beauty and charm of the young pair in love, but anti-monarchists were reminded anew of the foreign origins of their royal family. There was further joy over the birth of a daughter to the royal couple in July 1965. The constitution, however, gave precedence to male heirs, and the twenty-one cannon shots heralding the princess's birth would have been one hundred and one if the baby had been a boy. When the hundred and one shots did ring out for the birth of Crown

Prince Paul in May 1967 the country was already plunged in so deep a political abyss that some people wondered if the shots betokened something other than happiness.

Record of Papandreou as Prime Minister

Like that of Karamanlis, the government formed under Papandreou was oriented toward the West in international affairs, and the outlook in these matters would have been bright if it had not been for the increased bitterness between Greece and Turkey over Cyprus. Immediately on assuming office, Papandreou had to deal with the Cyprus fires which had flared up so ominously the preceding Christmas Eve. He showed himself a good tactician, as he frequently had in the past, managing not to antagonize Greek opinion while attaining, at least temporarily, a *modus vivendi* with the Turks.

His government was also faced with serious financial difficulties. It took office when there was already some discrepancy in the balance of payments. The special relationship of the United States and Greece was ending, and American funds, which had done so much since 1947 to make Greece's advance possible, had all but ceased by 1964. When the new prime minister requested further aid from the United States his appeal was turned down. Nor was the slack appreciably taken up by other countries. Large issues of Greek government bonds were not feasible until public confidence in the new government became established. Although Papandreou carried through plans for income tax reductions, and began to collect funds from the tax dodgers, he was unable to devise any arrangement which could prevent the inevitable difficulties arising from large new expenditures of public funds.

In his election campaign the new prime minister had overstated his economic case against Karamanlis. Many of the social and economic reforms advocated by Papandreou were long overdue, but when he took office he did little in the economic field that had not been begun by his predecessor. The emphasis and tempo were different. Karamanlis believed that, primarily because of the high costs involved, the government must make haste slowly in such matters as educational reform, and that expenditures for such purposes should come only after industry had begun to make a greater contribution to the national income. Although he continued to urge forward the industrialization of the country, Papandreou had promised the ordinary people of Greece a better life through a higher standard of living, including education, health, and welfare on an extended scale. Therefore he wanted to get ahead with social progress as quickly as possible and abandoned the Karamanlis program of attempted austerity.

Within a year after the elections regular government expenditures alone had risen by 18.5 per cent, some 40 per cent of which was attributable to increases in long-frozen wages and salaries. Spending for public education alone rose by an all-time record of 36 per cent in that same year. The most costly government plan, however, was the expanded program of subsidies for crops. Government warehouses were near bursting with crops purchased by the government over a period of years at prices above those of the international market. The politically advantageous but economically disastrous subsidies rose constantly in amount to individual farmers and in cost to the government in its deliberate attempt to raise farm income.

During Papandreou's term in office, imports climbed steadily but exports expanded at a pitifully slow rate so that the trade balance deteriorated notably. On the other hand, "invisibles" such as tourism, money sent home by Greeks abroad, and earnings from the shipping industry grew— except for a temporary slump in 1964 as a result of the Cyprus difficulties. Even when added to the receipts from exports, however, other growth was not sufficient to make up for the drain on foreign exchange.

While Papandreou reiterated his belief in industrialization and the necessity for increasing foreign investment in industry to bring in more foreign exchange and technical know-how, he insisted that the two largest foreign investors in Greece had been too generously treated by the National Radicals—as indeed many economists outside Greece believed. Changes in terms, forced in contracts renegotiated with Esso-Pappas and Aluminium de Grèce by the Papandreou government, did little to stimulate the atmosphere of trust necessary to secure further large-scale foreign investment.

As time passed, however, Papandreou, who had opposed the original contracts before he became prime minister, began to see some of the realities of the program of industrialization. He put new effort in programs to persuade investors to locate in provincial areas instead of in Athens wherever feasible, and to require that investors export a specified proportion of their output to bring in further foreign exchange.

Indications of disunity within the Center Union were quick to make themselves felt after Papandreou took office. It was reliably reported that two of the eight original Center Union leaders were unhappy because they were not given the posts they wanted and were temporarily put out of the party. Differences over policy became apparent. Constantine Mitsotakis, Minister of Finance, became deeply concerned over the government's financial difficulties and its serious balance of payments problems. On the other hand, the government was not grinding the mills of economic and social development fast enough to suit Elias Tsirimokas, who had been made Minister of the Interior. A number of other Center Union deputies began to see in Papandreou's control of the party much that they thought dictatorial and in his oratory much that appeared to them to be demagogic in appeal.

In political and administrative matters also there were differences within the party. Papandreou's policies seemed so transparently geared to his immediate political needs that long-range aims apparently were all but forgotten. To many observers he appeared more of a firebrand leader of noisy opposition than a prime minister in office, responsible for policy decisions and for their implementation. Carrying out policies was never Papandreou's strongest point. He reshuffled his cabinet constantly in accordance with his immediate political dictates and spent what experienced observers considered an inordinate amount of time beating dead political horses and digging in old records to prove that the National Radicals, and especially Karamanlis, had been utterly evil. All in all, the Papandreou government seemed to be squandering the political power it had secured with the elections of 1964.

Papandreou and Educational Reform

Even some of Papandreou's political enemies were willing to give him credit for his modernization of the educational system. Always interested in education, particularly since he had been Minister of Education and Religion some years previously, Papandreou made educational reform a leading plank in his campaign platforms and carried it through after he took office.

Papandreou was among the many who realized that the needs of Greece as a modern industrial nation were being poorly served by an educational system in which the young people spent so much of their school and university time on the study of Greek language, Greek history, Greek culture, and Greek Orthodox religion that they had little time for the newer subjects needed in the modern world. Greece's developing economy required scientists, mathematicians, economists, engineers, and others with specialized training who also had an understanding of modern foreign languages. While the country was woefully short of such professional graduates as well as those trained in management and business and of those with vocational training, its higher educational institutions were turning out a flood of such professionals as lawyers, doctors, and those trained in ancient languages and literature who were unable to find employment.

After his election, in addition to becoming prime minister, Papandreou took the portfolio as Minister of Education and Religion and used his Center Union majority to push an important educational reform law through Parliament in October 1964.[5] It revamped the existing system of traditional education, leaving change in vocational training to be undertaken in later laws.

Among its numerous forward-looking changes, the new law made the educational system completely free of cost and increased the number of years of required school attendance from six to nine, or from the twelfth to fifteenth year of age. The last three years of compulsory education were to be spent in a *gymnasium* (secondary school) for either general or vocational education. In a pattern not very different from that of junior and senior high schools in the United States, the required *gymnasium* years were to be followed by a three-year *lyceum* program—also free—available to those who passed the requisite entrance examinations.

The whole viewpoint toward languages was changed. The

people's language, *demotiki,* was to be made the operational language for all schools from the lowest to the highest, and the purist *katharévousa* was to be taught chiefly in the *gymnasia* and *lycea.* Basic in both was to be the study of modern Greek; classical Greek literature translated into modern *demotic* Greek; mathematics; history; physics; and either English or French. No longer were students to spend time learning ancient Greek grammar, syntax, and vocabulary rather than the contents of the ancient classics.

During Papandreou's term in office, resistance to educational change was still great. Many teachers, professors, state officers, and parents alike had acquired firm beliefs in the all-important values of the old classical education and frowned on science, engineering, and other technical subjects.

Communism in the 1960s

As prime minister, Papandreou pursued a more lenient policy than his predecessor in regard to imprisoned and exiled Communists. Although exact figures are hard to obtain, his government was reliably reported to have freed approximately the last thousand of those held in prison from the years of guerrilla warfare, and permitted as many as 12,000 individuals to return from other countries north of Greece.[6] Reports varied widely as to how many Communists still remained in exile and how organized they were for attack on Greece, but there were some in Communist countries whom Papandreou, never a Communist, for security reasons was unwilling to allow back in Greece.

After the Communist Party of Greece had been banned in 1947, the leaders of the organization went underground and fled the country, continuing to keep up the party structure and to direct subversive activities from outside. Within four years, the United Democratic Left had been formed in Greece as a cover for Communist activity. From its inception, the United Democratic Left included a number of people who were not, and never had been, Communists but who had become disillusioned with the progress of political and economic affairs within Greece and the handling of international affairs, notably Cyprus. It was always difficult, therefore, to assess with any degree of accuracy the actual Communist strength within the United Democratic Left.

From its founding the new party was headed by Ioannis Passalides. Born in the Caucasus in 1885, he studied medicine and was among the refugees who went to Greece in 1922. Passalides began to practice medicine in Thessaloniki within a year after his arrival, but he was apparently one of those who failed to adjust happily to his new surroundings and was susceptible to propaganda from the political far Left. He soon had become sufficiently involved in Leftist politics to be elected to Parliament. During the resistance in World War II he was active in the EAM.

It took time for the United Democratic Left to get under way. The memory of Communist horrors in the guerrilla fighting was still too vivid for an organization with even a tinge of Communism not to be anathema to most Greeks. In the year of its founding, the new party elected only ten deputies to Parliament. From 1951 onwards, however, the party appeared on the ballot in all elections, although not always alone or under its own name. In 1952, thanks to the personal strength of Field Marshal Papagos and the majority system of voting, the United Democratic Left secured no representation at all. Except for the special situation in 1958 when a combination of political circumstances brought the United Democratic Left over 900,000 votes, just under a quarter of all the valid ballots, the party vote ran somewhat over half a million or between 11 and 15 per cent of all the valid ballots cast.[7]

It was, however, impossible to tell how many of the United Democratic Left votes were actually Communist. It was estimated by a reliable source that the hard core of Communists accounted for only from 4 to 6 per cent of the vote of the whole United Democratic Left. The balance was a protest vote, of which there were many facets. A number of voters followed a political line which, more often than not, they failed to realize had been laid down by the Communist organization abroad, or if they did know it, they were more interested in other issues. Many without any Communist inclination followed the new party line because they were tired of the maneuvering of old-line politicians and political parties. Others voted the ticket because, for one reason or another, they were anti-American, anti-NATO, or had an especial interest in improving Greece's commercial relations with the countries of eastern Europe. Discontent with the handling of the Cyprus issue provided one of the strongest reasons for joining the protest vote.

The proposals of the United Democratic Left were often little concerned with Marxist problems but were devoted to social and economic affairs in fields that needed reform. In general, the party program was likely to find ready reception among those who lacked the good things of life and whose lot in Greece had been improved enough for them to realize how badly off they were. Emigrants who had become prosperous in western Europe returned home to see the lower standard of living in Greece and so inadvertantly—and sometimes deliberately—added to the discontent and willingness to listen to Communist-inspired ideas. Local politics also played a part. Possibly because of party discipline, candidates of Communist inclination were likely to have a reputation for more scrupulous honesty in local matters than many members of other parties. The increase in local United Democratic Left supporters in the municipal elections of July 1964 may be attributed in part to this reputation.

Communists usually found it suited their purposes better to act through other groups than political parties and so infiltrated organizations such as trade unions (which are politically oriented in Greece) and cooperatives. In addition, the Greek scene offered many opportunities for hidden propaganda among the young and poorly paid intellectuals. In the years after the end of the guerrilla warfare a generation had grown up that had not known the cruelty and horror of the long years of fighting with the Communists. Ardent nationalists, these young people were constantly and sometimes successfully wooed by the Communists in the United Democratic Left.

To aim their propaganda at the youth of Greece, the Communists founded the Democratic Youth Lambrakis in 1963. It was named after Gregorious Lambrakis, a United Democratic Left deputy killed in Thessaloniki in a street accident, whose death Communist sympathizers and a number of others attributed to a deliberate government action. He was made a martyr by the Communists, and the already growing ranks of the Democratic Youth Lambrakis grew still more. By 1966 it was estimated to number as many as 60,000, organized in some 4,500 Lambrakis clubs in even small villages.[8] Under the leadership of the Communist composer Mikis Theodorakis, whose music for "Zorba the Greek" made his name known throughout the world, the clubs provided entertainment, discussion groups, and pilgrimages to graves of Communist resistance victims. The clubs also organized demonstrations and became a thorn in the flesh of the Papandreou government. It, and later governments, tried to find a formula to break up the organization without violating constitutional provisions for freedom of speech.

Affairs have never gone smoothly within the ranks of the Communists, and they have always been divided by struggles for power. After Nikos Zakhariades had been released from the Dachau concentration camp by Allied forces in May 1945 and returned to Greece, he had had to fight to regain and keep his position of leadership. When the party had been banned in 1947 Zakhariades went underground and then fled the country. Always a Stalinist, he fell from grace in Communist circles, but it took three more years for him to be removed from the position of Secretary General of the Communist Party-in-exile. Finally called a "traitor," he and several of his followers were expelled from the party in 1957. According to reports, he went to live in Moscow and there, even at an advanced age, went to work in a factory.

After Zakhariades' political demise, the Communists, whether in exile or working unlabeled in the United Democratic Left, continued to suffer dissension. Meanwhile there had also been dispute within the ranks of the United Democratic Left between the old-line Communists and the newer non-Communist members who were not always willing to follow Communist directives.

From 1955 to 1964 there were altercations within the group as to how far it should work with, if not support, the parties of the center in order to weaken the position of the National Radicals. But the more bitter disagreements concerned international matters. The old scars of dispute between the supporters of Tito and of the U.S.S.R. remained after 1949. The battle between the Stalinist and anti-Stalinist elements was not stilled after Stalin's denigration. There were new disagreements between the pro-Chinese and those who continued to follow the line of the U.S.S.R. and among the supporters of different factions even within Communist China.

From the early 1950s to the late 1960s Greece was strongly divided as to whether greater leniency or greater severity should be shown toward known Communists and those of Communist inclination. It was the clear impression in Greece that the danger of a Communist uprising of serious proportions within Greece, or of a Communist military attack from abroad, had disappeared after the Communist defeat in 1949. People were reassured by increasingly good relations with Yugoslavia and finally Bulgaria, if not with Albania, and by the protective shield of Greece's membership in NATO. A segment of public opinion believed that the Communist party should once more be legalized within Greece because it would then appear clearly for what it was and not continue to masquerade, a wolf in sheep's clothing. If the Communist Party were legalized, the United Democratic Left would be shorn of its Communist direction and members and would be unable to survive. It was clear in any case that subversive activities carried on through channels other than political parties were more dangerous than those of an identifiable party organization.

It was also widely held that the improving economy and rising standard of living in Greece would prevent a large Communist increase as long as the nation maintained the governmental stability it had apparently achieved. Many people realized that Italy had managed to carry through an economic "miracle" despite an almost steady Communist vote of nearly a quarter of the total at each election, whereas in Greece the vote had only once, in a special set of circumstances in 1958, climed so high and usually hovered around 10 to 12 per cent.

There was, nevertheless, economic and political malaise,

and serious disturbance seemed possible to many Greeks. By and large the older people, with reason, hated and feared Communism because they had seen its devastation within their own country's borders. They were frightened by the circulation of rumors, for instance, that the United Democratic Left had increased its membership from 23,000 in 1963 to almost 90,000 four years later.[9] Other rumors concerned thousands of armed guerrillas waiting just outside the northern border to attack the country. A number of people were deeply disturbed by the idea of Communist infiltration of the Center Union. Although rumors had a part in the climax of the drama ahead, they were soon overwhelmed by the pressure of immediate events.

CHAPTER 9

After Papandreou the Deluge,

1965–1967

After Papandreou had been prime minister for somewhat over eighteen months—approximately the same length of time that King Constantine II had been on the throne—a storm over the powers of the king broke with full fury in mid-July 1965. What at first appeared to be a political argument between king and prime minister turned out to be a major crisis, involving, in the end, the existence of constitutional parliamentary government.

Because of the advent of his eldest son, Andreas Papandreou, in political affairs the political waters became muddied soon after Papandreou became prime minister. The role played by Andreas Papandreou was mysterious but important; it was one of the causes of the final catastrophe.

Andreas Papandreou

Born February 5, 1919, Andreas Papandreou was educated at Athens College, an American school, then attended the University of Athens while his father was in exile under the Metaxas regime. Leaving Greece in late 1939, reportedly because of possible arrest for his activities in an attempted overthrow of Metaxas, Andreas Papandreou went to the

United States. He remained there for the next twenty years, acquiring a doctoral degree in economics from Harvard University, and subsequently teaching there. Becoming an American citizen, he was commissioned in the United States Navy in World War II, and served as technical adviser at the 1944 financial and monetary conference at Bretton Woods. He married an American-born wife and held various university teaching posts, going finally to the University of California as professor and head of department in 1955.

At the invitation of Prime Minister Karamanlis, the younger Papandreou returned to Greece in 1959 to establish the Center of Economic Research, a semi-governmental and semi-private research and planning institution in Athens, financed partly by Greek and partly by American funds. When his father was seeking office and it appeared he would become prime minister, the son decided to remain in Greece and enter politics. By election to Parliament, for which Greek citizenship is a constitutional prerequisite,[1] he was deemed under the regulations and constitutional interpretation of the United States to have violated American law and so lost his American citizenship. After his father was appointed prime minister, the younger Papandreou was made minister to the prime minister, and thus became his father's chief assistant and adviser, if not *alter ego*. Later he was given the important post of alternate minister of coordination. Under suspicion of an unproved scandal involving the award of a government contract and the subject of other rumors and charges about his political activities, he resigned his post in November 1964. He was back in the same position the following April.

As the ministry of coordination involved knowledge of economics and especially planning, Andreas Papandreou was generally regarded as well-fitted for his post by long experience in dealing with such problems. But many thinking people

objected to his ever-deepening involvement in Greek politics
and foreign affairs, beginning with difficult Cyprus negotiations, which were not part of his field of experience. Others
objected to his obvious grooming as successor to his elderly
father. The most frequent charge was that his political orientation was moving toward the United Democratic Left, although whether because of belief or possible political
advantage was not clear. Finally came his rumored connection
with an army conspiracy which was destined to precipitate
his father's political downfall.

The "Aspida" Affair

Among the more serious rumors circulating about the
younger Papandreou was that indicating his involvement in
the army plot. On various occasions before World War II
the armed forces, in the persons of various officers, had been
deeply involved in republican politics and in attempts to
make Greece a republic. But after World War II and the
guerrilla fighting following it, the armed forces, of which the
king was the commander-in-chief,[2] had become the defender
not only of his person but also of the ideology of the monarchy. With renewed emphasis after Greece's entry into
NATO, the armed forces had also become the bulwark of
defense against the possibility of renewed Communist outbreak in Greece. American influence and the large amounts
of American military aid had not been without repercussions
on the situation. But the officers corps had been tradition-
alists by selection and training, reinforced in their attitude
by the long ascendency of the political parties headed by
Papagos and Karamanlis, generally regarded as pro-mon-
archist and conservative.

Under the circumstances, and in view of the considerable

history of the armed forces' involvement in politics, Prime Minister Papandreou appeared anxious to penetrate the army with his type of liberal political thinking. Accordingly, in late June 1965, he made a statement in Parliament announcing the planned removal of all officers of doubtful loyalty to his government. He subsequently transferred a number of officers to posts away from Athens, presumably so that these men might be removed further from the influence of the crown.

At about the same time a secret organization, the *Aspida* (a name meaning *shield* but derived from the initial Greek letters for "Officers Save the Country and Its Ideals of Democracy and Meritocracy"), was discovered in the army and reported in the press. The organization was reportedly trying to infiltrate the army with republican if not socialist and even Communist ideas. A number of sources indicated that Andreas Papandreou was involved and was trying to use the *Aspida* not only as a means of infiltrating the armed forces with "left-wing ideology" but also of building up a personal junta.

The persistent charges remained unproven, and the younger Papandreou remained a man of mystery. By his enemies he was "regarded as a man who wanted to be the Gamal Abdol Nasser of Athens and by his friends as a Western European progressive."[3] Abroad as well as in Greece he became the subject of much speculation. He was characterized, for instance, in an article by C. L. Sulzberger in the *New York Times* as an "engaging but arrogantly ambitious power seeker, increasingly linked to the far-out left."[4] Other qualified observers, and particularly those who had been associated with him at work in either the United States or Greece, had a different verdict.[5] Various ones who knew his work at the Center of Economic Research in Athens were filled with praise for his studies and plans to develop the Greek economy.

Struggle between King Constantine II and
Prime Minister Papandreou

In his attempt to purge the armed forces of elements
opposed to his government the elder Papandreou lacked the
backing of his defense minister, Patros Garofoulias, a member
of the Center Union but also a trusted admirer of the King.
Papandreou requested the minister to resign and told the
King of his request and of his wish to take over the defense
portfolio himself, although he was already minister of education and religion as well as prime minister. The implication
was clear that Papandreou as defense minister might easily
protect his son in a forthcoming investigation of the *Aspida*.
The King refused to sign the decree dismissing Garofoulias,
but reliable reports later indicated that he would have signed
if anyone but the prime minister himself were to be minister
of defense.

Papandreou, believing that as prime minister he had the
power to decide who was to constitute his cabinet, told the
King he would present his formal resignation the day following the discussion if he were not allowed to appoint
himself minister of defense. In the King's view, the statement
in itself constituted a resignation without need for presentation of a formal document; the prime minister believed he
was "dismissed" by the King, who immediately went about
finding a successor.

Papandreou insisted that he had a majority in Parliament
and so the King must immediately reappoint him or dissolve Parliament and call new elections. Both of these the
King refused to do. Under the constitution of 1952, the
monarch had the undoubted right to "appoint and dismiss"
his ministers, although the right of appointment was limited

by the need for a vote of confidence in Parliament.[6] The King therefore was constitutionally allowed to summon anyone he chose for prime minister, and the practical problem was to appoint someone who could wend his way through the labyrinth of Parliament and come out safely at the end. Tradition had it that the king chose the leader of the political party with the largest number of seats, who in this case would be Papandreou. But kings in the past had not always chosen the leader of the party. After the death of Papagos in 1955, for example, it was generally expected that the office would go to Deputy Prime Minister Kanellopoulos, senior in command of Papagos' Greek Rally. Instead, Constantine Karamanlis was chosen. Although a cabinet minister and member of the same party, he was not a well-known leader in it. Thus, in terms of precedence, King Constantine II was within his rights in refusing to reappoint Papandreou as prime minister, but in practical terms Papandreou's large majority in Parliament could not be dismissed lightly.

The constitution did not make it clear whether a king, in appointing a minister, had the determining voice in selecting him. Papandreou argued that cabinet appointments must be made on the authority of the prime minister but with the advice of the king. In this view, the king was limited to making suggestions and had no power to decide who was— or was not—to hold any particular cabinet post. In other words, Papandreou saw the powers of the prime minister in this regard as much the same as in Britain, where "few dictators enjoy such a measure of autocratic power as is enjoyed by the British prime minister while he is in the process of making up his cabinet."[7] In the silence of the Greek constitution, Papandreou assumed that the progress of constitutional affairs in Greece had approximated that in Britain. He did not consider differences in development of the two-party system in Britain and the multi-party arrangement of Greece nor the role of the king in each country.

The king's power to dismiss included the right to demand the resignation of a government of which he disapproved, even if it had a parliamentary majority. Although many constitutional scholars regarded this as a power to be used only in extreme circumstances, it had been used by kings who believed they had an absolute right of dismissal. When King Constantine I demanded the resignation of Prime Minister Venizelos twice during the year 1915 over the same issue of foreign policy, Venizelos had a majority in Parliament and insisted that the King was exceeding his powers because the issue had not changed. The electorate had expressed their approval of the prime minister not once but twice by returning him to Parliament after his first dismissal.

In the present case Papandreou had received a vote of confidence, and it had never been overridden by a vote of no-confidence. The constitution required that a government "must enjoy the confidence of Parliament,"[8] and this Papandreou's government, with its large majority, amply did. Papandreou reiterated over and over that as the Center Union had never lost Parliament's confidence, it was still the legally constituted government in which the King had no right to interfere.

Papandreou insisted that if the King did not reappoint him, Parliament must be dissolved so that the electorate could express its views at a new election. In other words, the ex-prime minister held that under the circumstances the King was required to order dissolution. The constitution of 1952, however, embodied certain safeguards. To prevent a monarch from dissolving Parliament and ruling permanently without it, the constitution required the king to convoke Parliament in ordinary session once a year[9] and call it into extraordinary session whenever he deemed desirable. Although the monarch had the right, once only, to suspend Parliament's work, the suspension could not exceed thirty days.[10] On expiration of a term of Parliament, elections were required within forty-five days on decree of the king.[11] The ministers and Parliament had the power to initiate and approve legislation and the crown was forbidden to promulgate any law unless signed by the minister in charge of its particular subject matter. In other words, the ministers were responsible but the king was not.[12] Even in emergencies, the king was not allowed to issue decrees with the force of law without the concurring opinion of a special committee of deputies set up at the beginning of each session of Parliament.[13]

The constitution further provided that the crown had the right to dissolve Parliament, and nothing in the constitutional wording indicated what circumstances might require dissolution.[14] The matter was left to the king for decision. If, however, he decided on dissolution, he was required to embody in the decree a call for new elections to be held within forty-five days, the convocation of the new Parliament within three months.[15]

The storm had broken. The crown had become as deeply involved in politics as when the King's grandfather, King Constantine I, had been on the throne. Like his grandfather, he believed his power to dismiss was absolute, and included the right to demand the resignation of a prime minister and government of which he disapproved, even though it had a majority in Parliament. The first King Constantine had piled Ossa on Pelion in the Venizelos case; the second King Constantine was prevented by his own actions and the tide of events from dismissing Papandreou twice. Unlike his grandfather, King Constantine II did not have a history of serious dispute with a prime minister as did King Constantine I with Prime Minister Venizelos. Nor did King Constantine II immediately dissolve Parliament and call for new elections as his grandfather had done. In 1965 a parliamentary majority had become a matter of even more serious import in a democratic country than it had been fifty years previously. The years since 1915, furthermore, had seen one crowned head after another dissappear from the thrones of Europe.

Both the King and the Prime Minister made serious mistakes in their public relations, if not in their legal actions. All but his most devoted admirers thought that King Constantine II was inexperienced in political judgment because of his youth, and possibly ill-advised, and that apparently he had forgotten the unfortunate legacy of his grandfather. Although considered courageous, the young King was widely accused of having wounded the national *philotimo*.[16] A series of vehement demonstrations followed the Papandreou removal; how far they were Communist-inspired was an open question. A comment in *The World Today,* published by the Royal Institute of International Affairs in London, expressed the view that "it seems probable" that in 1965 and subsequent demonstrations, "the majority of the participants were not Communist sympathizers but radicals seeking social and economic reforms through stable government; an end to corruption in public life; a turn away from dependence on the United States and, possibly, towards neutrality for Greece; and, without prejudice to the particular occupant of the throne, an end to the institution of monarchy."[17]

When he was no longer prime minister, Papandreou took pains to make it clear that he had no desire to see the monarchy liquidated and insisted on nothing more than a British-type relationship between the monarch and the prime minister in which the king reigned and the government ruled as the representative of the people. His son Andreas advocated the same type of government but did it more vehemently, reiterating the theme that the Greek people should no longer "tolerate" a king who wished to rule as well as reign.

In the eyes of many people, the elder Papandreou failed to learn during his long political career that the essence of politics is compromise not only for votes but also for the actual progress of the country. At the very least, he had again started the old whirligig of splits, divisions, regroupings, and instability in the politics of Greece. More important, by their intransigence, both the King and Papandreou had played major roles in the fall of parliamentary government that was to come in the spring of 1967.

Granting the King's involvement in politics up to the hilt, he had various alternatives. First, he could have acceded to to one or the other of Papandreou's demands, that is, he could have reinstated him or called new elections. Either of the possibilities would have led to a diminution of the royal image, if not worse. Second, the King could have appointed a non-political prime minister from outside the party structure to head a government of national unity. But this too would have flouted the majority principle and would have been only a temporary expedient, showing that all others had failed, and itself ultimately leading to further elections. Third, the King might have imposed his will by the use of the army.

Attempts to Form Another Government, 1965

Although the King failed to follow the tradition of choosing as prime minister the leader of the political party with the largest number of deputies in Parliament, he did rely on the precedent that another member of the same party might be chosen. Unwilling to reappoint the leader of the Center Union, the King continued to try to find a prime minister from the same party. In looking for a successor within the Center Union ranks, the King immediately chose Georgios Athanasiadis-Novas from the more conservative ranks of the party, but was rebuffed when his candidate failed to muster a vote of confidence. Meanwhile, Papandreou was using his own considerable oratorical and maneuvering skill to persuade the electorate that he should be reinstated, or else that the matter should be decided by an immediate vote. Papandreou's popularity was such that he had reason to believe that his already large parliamentary majority might be increased if elections were held immediately.

As the situation wore on, Papandreou's popularity apparently continued great in the country at large but began to decline within his own Center Union ranks in Parliament. Deserters from among his deputies became numerous. In any event, a large group of deputies realized that if Papandreou did not return to power, their own political futures might be damaged by continuing to follow his leadership. Others believed that, if a compromise were not found, Greece might lose much of what it had gained in the years of stable politics, and that even the economy might be jeopardized. Still others saw in the noisy turbulence of those days a signal of possible Communist resurgence by violent means.

The King, mindful that the Center Union was still the strongest party in Parliament, continued his endeavors to find a candidate among its members. After consultation with leaders representing all shades of political opinion, he turned to Stephanos Stephanopoulos, deputy prime minister under Papandreou. In a last-ditch attempt to keep Center Union discipline, Stephanopoulos agreed to accept the mandate only if the party caucus approved. Still loyal to Papandreou, the caucus turned down the request. On his third try, the King went to the left of the Center Union and selected the socialist Elias Tsirimokos, a defector from Papandreou. He too failed to make the grade.

A Government Finally Formed

Finally enough deputies had deserted the Center Union to join with other parties, notably the National Radicals, to form a government. In a dramatic session of Parliament on September 24, 1965, with all deputies present and voting (except one who was ill, and even he sent in his vote), Stephanos Stephanopoulos, by then having broken with the Center Union, pulled through as prime minister with four votes to spare. The votes of all the forty-five who had deserted Papandreou and the Center Union, plus the ninety-nine National Radicals and the eight Progressives, made the slim victory (152-148) possible. Led by the elderly but still erect Papandreou, who entered the hall only to vote *no* in the vote of confidence and then left, the one hundred and twenty-six remaining Center Union stalwarts joined the twenty-two members of the United Democratic Left in casting the negative ballots. The bitterness of the old man had become so great that he was willing to accept the Communist-sponsored party as a working companion. Yet only two years previously he had turned down their support. But no one, not even his worst enemies, accused the elder Papandreou of having become a Communist.

The Political Treadmill in Motion Again

The Stephanopoulos government, formed by such a narrow margin, was indeed a strange one, depending for its life on the support of the parties defeated in the preceding election. The defectors from the Center Union who had joined the government believed their position might be strengthened by organizing themselves as a new party—a time-honored device in Greek politics. So in the early summer of 1966 they formed their new organization under the name of the Liberal Democratic Center (*Philaleftheron Dimokratikon Kentron,* PDK). But all it accomplished was to identify them.

Although the Stephanopoulos government was designed as a stopgap and its four-vote margin in Parliament gave it no room for negotiation, it did manage to stay in office for fifteen months, an incredibly long period under the circumstances. The government did not prove to be as unavailing as such stopgap arrangements often are; its accomplishment was to consolidate gains already made. First, a measure of economic confidence lost under Papandreou was briefly restored. The government managed to lessen the danger of serious inflation and for the moment curbed the heavy speculation in gold which had come immediately after the 1965 crisis. Economic development, which had slowed down after mid-1965, quickened its pace. Second, without fanfare, the government continued to carry on Greek-Turkish negotiations over Cyprus, which at least kept the governments of Greece and Turkey talking together instead of fighting each other. Third, public order was maintained in a time of rising political emotions, although accusations were frequent that this had been accomplished by intimidation of opposing groups.

During those fifteen months, nevertheless, the parliamentary machinery ground to a standstill. Deputies were slow to take action on urgently needed legislation because in all parties the future was so unclear that a turn of the political wheel might make them wish they had acted differently, if they had acted at all. In education, for instance, the law en-

acted by Parliament in 1964, increasing the years of compulsory education and changing the educational curriculum
in important ways, languished with little or no implementation. Because the law was regarded as a child of the Papandreou government the opposing parties took the stand that
the whole law was political, and so classrooms and labora-
tory space, although urgently necessary, remained unprovided,
and textbooks were unprinted.

Unable to carry through a normal legislative program, the
government spent much energy on the continued investigation of the *Aspida* affair and on the personal history of
Andreas Papandreou. Many observers believed that the constant attacks on him served to build him up as a political
force, although "his only obvious qualifications for this role
[were] his father's name and a bold left-of-center anti-
monarchist posture."[18]

Still More Governments, 1966–1967

Gradually the National Radicals became restive in the government of which they formed the largest part. Not always
consulted for decisions, they came to believe that they might
possibly better their position by going to the polls again.
Some saw clearly the anomaly of a government based on
parties held together by the wishes of the king and on opposition to the largest party in Parliament. Accordingly, the National Radical leader, Panayotis Kanellopoulos, a man of
moderate views and background of distinguished service to
his country, withdrew his party's ninety-nine votes from
support of the government because new elections were not
forthcoming. Requesting a transition government to hold
elections within the next six months, Prime Minister Stephanopoulos resigned.

On the necessity of holding elections, the National Radicals and the Center Union were agreed. Both therefore joined in a vote of confidence for an interim, non-political government under Ioannis Paraskevopoulos, governor of the Bank of Greece and a man noted for his impartiality. His government took over the reins on December 24, 1966. Before the vote a flurry of disagreement between the Papandreous, *père et fils,* indicated to many people that the senior Papandreou's vote for confirmation of the government was a bid for the support of the conservative wing of the Center Union, while his son's objection was taken to please its left wing. It was true that the two men had not been in entire agreement over the constitutional question. Throughout the period of ever-changing governments, the elder Papandreou had no wish to have the elections turn into a referendum on the monarchy. His son's bombastic utterances were less clear on the point, although sometimes sounding fiercely anti-monarchist and the next minute less so. Only the Communists and fellow travelers apparently really wanted the issue to be brought into the campaign.

Andreas Papandreou was the rock on which the ship foundered. The Paraskevopoulos government lasted a short fourteen weeks before the Prime Minister handed in his resignation on March 30, 1967. During the life of that government, the public prosecutor had attempted to have the younger Papandreou's immunity as deputy lifted so that a civil suit could be brought against him for conspiracy to commit high treason because of his suspected part in the *Aspida* affair. Some months earlier, court martial proceedings had been begun against the army officers involved in the plan to infiltrate the military forces with republican, socialist, and possibly even Communist adherents. On March 10, fifteen of the twenty-eight officers involved were sentenced to imprisonment for terms varying from two to eighteen years, and thirteen were acquitted.

Rumors had become insistent that Andreas Papandreou had been the civilian leader of the group. Yet, as a deputy in Parliament, he was entitled to immunity under the constitution of 1952. As in most legislative bodies, it was forbidden to prosecute or question a deputy for any opinion or vote given by him in the performance of his duties.[19] But the more important immunity for Andreas Papandreou was that which forbade the prosecution, arrest, or imprisonment of a deputy during a session of Parliament without its permission.[20] Nor was it allowable for any deputy to be personally detained for four weeks after the end of a parliamentary term.[21] Since the constitution required elections to be called within forty-five days there was an interval during which a suit could have been brought against the younger Papandreou. The reason appeared all too clear why the Center Union introduced legislation extending the legal immunity of a deputy for the whole period between the dissolution of Parliament and new elections. The parties in the government, spurred by the National Radicals, refused to accept such a plan and so the Paraskevopoulos government fell.

By this time the possible combinations to form a government were exhausted. The King hoped that one composed of all parties might succeed. When discussions showed this to be impossible, the last refuge appeared to be a minority government composed of National Radicals as the largest opposition party. In the hope that Panayotis Kanellopoulos—a man highly respected even by his political enemies—could form a government and then persuade the splinter parties to cooperate long enough to enact legislation under which the elections could be carried on, the King turned to him. The bait held out to the smaller groups was an arrangement under a system of proportional representation by which they would be able to secure a proportionately larger number of seats. But the bait was not attractive enough, and they refused to take it.

In the eyes of many, the King's choice of a minority opposition government of National Radicals to conduct the elections was another serious mistake at a time when feelings were running high. After four days of fruitless negotiation, Kanellopoulos failed to secure the agreement of the small parties. The already murky waters were further clouded by Papandreou's refusal to attend an all-party leaders' meeting. Utterly frustrated, Kanellopoulos gave up the battle on April 3. Parliament was dissolved on April 14, and to bring them within the forty-five day constitutional requirement elections were called for May 28, just forty-three days later. As no new electoral law had been passed, the electoral system that had been used in 1964 was to provide the machinery again. By this time, there was little doubt in anyone's mind that Papandreou and the Center Union would win the victory on May 28, and it was believed that his majority would be even larger than before.

The Dénouement: the Coup of April 21, 1967

By mid-April events moved rapidly to a climax. No choices were left to the King except that of a Center Union government under Papandreou, which the King had steadily refused to countenance since 1965. The crisis was now one of the whole system of parliamentary government, which might be said to have broken down if indeed it had ever worked smoothly. Rumors continued to spread that the King and high officers of the armed forces might attempt a coup and royal dictatorship. But when the coup did come, in the early hours of April 21, and the tanks moved in the streets of Athens, the King appeared to most observers to have had no part in it. The careful safeguards of the constitution of 1952 against the assumption of power by the King, even in a crisis, without the agreement of Parliament were swept away.[22] A group of army colonels had stepped in as the military had done so many times before in Greece, and parliamentary constitutional government was at an end.

Notes

Chapter 1: The Setting

1. *United States Aid to Greece, 1947–1966*

Economic	$1,895.1 million
Military	$1,854.3 million
Total	$3,749.4 million

Of this total, $3,410.9 million consisted of grants and $338.4 million were loans. Technical Assistance and Supporting Assistance programs were terminated in 1962 and major economic aid was ended in 1964 because the Agency for International Development considered Greece to be an outstanding example of a successful assistance program. Military aid was continued; the level for the year July 1, 1966–June 30, 1967 was $64,981,000. (*Letter to the authors from the Department of State, Agency for International Development,* September 18, 1967.)

2. *Growth Rate of Gross National Product, 1963–1966* (at 1958 prices)

1963	8.0%
1964	8.6%
1965	7.2%
1966	8.2%

Statistical Yearbook of Greece, 1965 (Athens: National Statistical Service of Greece, 1966). *Greece Today,* National Bank of Greece, Athens, January 1967, p. 18.

3. *Growth of Gross National Income* (in percentages)

1964	8.6%
1965	7.2%
1966	8.2% (also given as 8.4%)

Report for the Year 1966, Bank of Greece, Athens, 1967, p. 12; see also *Report of the Chairman of the Board of Directors,* Commercial Bank of Greece, Athens, 1967, p. 30.

4. *Farm and City Per Capita Income, 1958 and 1965* (National Average, 1958, $334; 1965, $495)

	Farm	% Farm Increase	City	% City Increase
1958	$220		$437	
1965	$285	30%	$675	40%

5. Georges Langrod, *Reorganization of Public Administration in Greece* (Paris: Organization for Economic Cooperation and Development, 1964), pp. 19-20.

Since 1864 Greece has adopted new constitutions or modified older ones, in 1911, 1927 (constitution of the republic), 1935 (restoration of the monarchy), and January 1, 1952 (largely abrogated by the coup d'état of April 21, 1967).

6. Lord Campion et al., *Parliament, A Survey* (London: George Allen and Unwin, 1952), p. 57.

7. Margaret Mead, ed., *Cultural Patterns and Technical Change.* Prepared by UNESCO (New York: Mentor Books, 1955), p. 61.

8. In the present book the city is referred to as Constantinople until the official Turkish change of name after World War I. After that, it is called Istanbul, with no political implications concerning the use of the names.

The word Ottoman is used rather than Turkish in discussing the period to the end of the Ottoman Empire with the Treaty of Lausanne because, while the Empire lasted, it included other groups in addition to Turks.

9. All other religions account for only some 2 per cent of the population. *Unclassified Data,* U.S. Embassy, Athens, February 1965.

10. Constitution of 1952, Art. 16.

11. Moses Hadas, *Hellenistic Culture: Fusion and Diffusion* (New York: Columbia University Press, 1959), p. 1.

Chapter 2: The People and Their Background

1. Winston S. Churchill, *Triumph and Tragedy*, Vol. VI of *The Second World War* (Boston: Houghton Mifflin Co., 1953), p. 325.

2. H. C. Darby, "Mediaeval and Turkish Greece," in W. A. Heurtley, H. C. Darby, C. W. Crawley, and C. W. M. Woodhouse, *A Short History of Modern Greece* (Cambridge: University Press, 1965), p. 46. The authors are heavily indebted to this book, especially for parts of Chapter 2 and Chapter 3 of their own book.

3. Report of a Venetian commissioner, quoted in "Crete," *Encyclopaedia Britannica*, Eleventh Edition, 1909-1911, p. 427.

4. Alfred Zimmern, *The Greek Commonwealth*, 5th ed. (Oxford: Clarendon Press, 1931), p. 19.

5. Discussion of Cyprus is not included in the present book. See Appendix to Chapter 3.

6. For history of the siege, see Steven Runciman, *The Fall of Constantinople, 1453* (Cambridge: University Press, 1965), *passim*, esp. pp. 15 and 99.

7. Nicholas Kaltchas, *Introduction to the Constitutional History of Modern Greece* (New York: Columbia University Press, 1940), p. 11.

8. Patrick Leigh Fermor, *Mani: Travels in the Southern Peloponnese* (London: John Murray, 1958), *passim*, esp. p. 12.

Chapter 3: Growth of the Nation

1. Bulletin Mensuel de Statistique, No. 1 (Athens: Statistical Service, January 1926), quoted by Alec P. Alexander, *Greek Industrialists* (Athens: Center of Planning and Economic Research, 1964, Research Monograph Series 12), p. 57.

2. Nikos Kazantzakis, *Journey to the Morea* (New York: Simon and Schuster, 1965), p. 165.

3. Nikos Kazantzakis, *Report to Greco* (Oxford: Bruno Cassirer, 1965), p. 106.

4. See Eleutherios Prevelakis, "Eleutherios Venizelos and the Balkan Wars," in *Balkan Studies* (Thessaloniki: Institute of Balkan Studies, 1966), Vol. 7, No. 2, p. 378.

5. Margaret Mead, ed., *Cultural Patterns and Social Change*, pp. 59-60.

6. Patrick Leigh Fermor, *Roumeli Travels in Northern Greece* (London: John Murray, 1966), p. 30. For more detailed discussion of the Vlachs and Sarakatsáns, see J. K. Campbell, *Honour, Family and Patronage* (Oxford: Clarendon Press, 1964), Ch. 1, *passim*.

7. Fermor, *Roumeli*, p. 31.

8. Darby, "Mediaeval and Turkish Greece," in Heurtley et al., *A Short History of Modern Greece*, p. 46.

9. Evangelos Kefos, *Nationalism and Communism in Macedonia* (Thessaloniki: Institute for Balkan Studies, 1964), pp. 5, 186-87.

10. According to the 1961 census, out of a population of 1,700,000 in Greek Macedonia, only 41,017 spoke primarily a Slavic language. Kefos, *Nationalism*, p. 5.

11. *Ibid.*

Chapter 4: *Monarchy, Republics, and Dictatorships before World War II*

1. Nicholas Kaltchas, *Introduction to the Constitutional History of Modern Greece*, p. 83.

2. C. W. Crawley, "Modern Greece, 1821–1930," in Heurtley et al., *A Short History of Modern Greece*, p. 101.

3. King Othon (1833–1862) was Greece's only Bavarian king. After him came six kings of the dynasty of the Glücksborgs of Denmark: George I (1863–1913); Constantine I (1913–1917 and 1920–1922); Alexander (1917–1920); George II (1922–1924 and 1935–1947); Paul I (1947–1964); Constantine II (1964–   ).

4. Donna W. Dontas, *Greece and the Great Powers, 1863–1875* (Thessaloniki: Institute of Balkan Studies, 1966), p. 12.

5. Kaltchas, *Introduction to Constitutional History*, p. 141.

6. Crawley, *Modern Greece*, p. 109.

7. Kaltchas, *Introduction to Constitutional History*, p. 135.

8. Edward S. Forster, *A Short History of Modern Greece, 1821–1956* (London: Methuen and Co., 1958), p. 160.

9. *Ibid.*

10. *Ibid.*, pp. 162-63.

11. Venizelos' Statement before Parliament, May 15, 1933, quoted by D. George Kousoulas, *Revolution and Defeat, the Story of the Greek Communist Party* (London: Oxford University Press, 1965), p. 85.

Chapter 5: Parliaments, Political Parties, and the Long Dictatorship before World War II

1. Art. 44, quoted by Kaltchas, *Introduction to the Constitutional History of Modern Greece,* p. 31.
2. Edward S. Forster, *A Short History of Modern Greece, 1821–1956,* p. 19.
3. Kaltchas, *Introduction to Constitutional History,* especially Chs. IV and V for history of the period. See also S. M. Sophocles, *A History of Greece* (Thessaloniki: Institute of Balkan Studies, 1961), *passim.*
4. For pre-World War I history of the political parties (in English), see esp. Forster, *A Short History of Modern Greece;* Heurtley et al., *A Short History of Modern Greece,* Chapter by C. W. Crawley, "Modern Greece, 1821–1939"; Kousoulas, *Revolution and Defeat;* Bickham Sweet-Escott, *Greece—a Political and Economic Survey* (London: Royal Institute of International Affairs, 1954); C. W. M. Woodhouse, *Apple of Discord* (London: Hutchinson and Co., 1948). The last volume deals primarily with the period of World War II.
5. In the 1926 elections, out of the total of 286 seats, the Liberals won 143, the Populists 127, and the Popular Front 10; a scattering of independents secured 6 seats. Kousoulas, *Revolution and Defeat,* pp. 48 and 65.
6. In the elections of March 5, 1933, the Liberals secured 111 seats and the Populists 131, while the United Front, together with other small parties, got 6 seats. In the elections of the preceding September 25, the Liberals had obtained 102 seats, the Populists 96, the Progressive Republicans 15, and various scattered groups 40, of which 7 belonged to the Popular Front. Forster, *A Short History,* p. 180; Kousoulas, *Revolution and Defeat,* p. 82.
7. In the elections of June 9, 1935, 243 Populists were elected, 37 followers of General Kondylis, 7 Metaxas followers, and 6 independents. Although the Liberals of Venizelos had been ordered to abstain, a total vote of 1,030,362 was cast, indicating that some Liberals voted. Forster, *A Short History,* p. 189.
8. Kousoulas, *Revolution and Defeat,* p. 96.

9. In the elections of January 26, 1936, the Populists and the Popular-Radical Party (of General Kondylis) won 582,940 votes or 45.6 per cent of the total of 1,270,085 votes and 143 seats; the Liberals, supported by the Republicans and Agrarians, secured 44 per cent and 142 seats, of which 127 were credited to the Liberals; the Popular Front, with 73,441 votes, or 4 per cent of the total, secured 15 seats; the small Peasant Party got 1 seat. Kousoulas, *Revolution and Defeat*, p. 97.

10. Fifth World Congress of the *Comintern*, Abridged Report, p. 268, quoted by Kousoulas, *Revolution and Defeat*, p. 64.

11. Kousoulas, *Revolution and Defeat*, p. 36.

12. Crawley, in Heurtley et al., *A Short History*, p. 129.

Chapter 6: The Dreadful Decade, 1940–1950

1. I. McD. G. Stewart, *The Struggle for Crete, 20 May–1 June, 1941* (London: Oxford University Press, 1966), p. 18.

2. *Ibid.*, p. 67.

3. Edgar O'Ballance, *The Greek Civil War 1944–1949* (London: Faber and Faber, 1966), p. 50.

4. *Ibid.*, p. 82.

5. Kousoulas, *Revolution and Defeat*, p. 150.

6. A clear picture of Grivas emerges in his autobiography, *The Memoirs of General Grivas*, ed. by Charles Foley (New York, Frederick A. Praeger, 1964), p. 18.

7. O'Ballance, *The Greek Civil War*, p. 79.

8. See Churchill, *Triumph and Tragedy*, Ch. 19, "Christmas in Greece," *passim*.

9. Sir Reginald Leeper, *When Greek Meets Greek* (London: Chatto and Windus, 1950), p. 116.

10. Sweet-Escott, *Greece*, p. 53.

11. Of the 354 seats of which Parliament then consisted, the Populists and other monarchists secured 231; the followers of Papandreou and Sophoklis Venizelos (Liberals) 67; Republicans 51; and smaller groups secured scattered seats.

12. O'Ballance, *Greek Civil War*, p. 129.

13. C. W. M. Woodhouse, Foreword to O'Ballance, *Greek Civil War*, p. 15. See also his foreword to Kousoulas, *Revolution and Defeat*, p. vii.

14. In the 1950 elections, the number of seats in Parliament was

reduced to 250. Of these, the Populists secured 62, the Liberals 36, the National Coalition of the Center 45, the Democratic Socialists under Papandreou 35, and the Democratic Front 18. Two minor parties, the National Party of General Zervas got 7 seats, and the Progressive Party of Markezinis, 1. Kousoulas, *Revolution and Defeat,* p. 273.

Chapter 7: Years of Stability, 1952–1961

1. In the 1951 elections, the Greek Rally secured 114 of the 250 seats of which Parliament was composed; the National Progressive Union of the Center secured 74 seats, the Liberals 57, and the United Democratic Left 10. Forster, *A Short History,* p. 235.

2. William Hardy McNeill, *Greece: American Aid in Action, 1947–1956* (New York: Twentieth Century Fund, 1957), p. 48.

3. Theodore A. Couloumbis, *Greek Political Reaction to American and NATO Influences* (New Haven: Yale University Press, 1966), p. 52.

4. *Ibid.,* p. 54.   5. *Ibid.,* p. 55.

6. With just 49.22 per cent of the valid vote of 1,591,807 in 1952, the Greek Rally secured 247 of the 300 seats; the association of Liberals and the National Progressive Union of the Center 51; and Independents 2. For election results and party line-ups from 1953–1964, see Couloumbis, *Political Reaction,* Appendix E, *passim.* All figures below are from that Appendix.

7. *Ibid.,* p. 89.

8. With 47.48 per cent of the valid vote of 1,594,112 in 1956, the National Radicals secured 165 seats; the Democratic Union with 25,895 votes more than the National Radicals, or 48.15 per cent of the total, got 132 seats, of which 15 belonged to the United Democratic Left and 3 to Independents.

9. (1) The National Radical Union; (2) the Union of the Populist Party, made up of discontented conservatives; (3) the Liberals headed by Sophoklis Venizelos and Georgios Papandreou; (4) the Progressive Agrarian Democratic Union, made up of the Progressives, followers of Markezinis; what was left of the National Progressive Union of the Center; the Agrarian Party, interested in the views of Greek farmers only; the Democratic Party, a social-welfare oriented group; (5) the United Democratic Left. See Couloumbis, *Political Reaction,* p. 120.

10. Of the 3,847,785 ballots cast in 1958, the National Radical Union received 1,583,885, or 41.16 per cent of the vote, and 171 seats out of the 300 total; the United Democratic Left got 838,902, or 24.43 per cent of the vote, and 79 seats; the two center parties (Liberals and the Progressive Agrarian Democratic Union) together got 1,204,231 or 31.29 per cent of the vote, but only 46 seats. A minor coalition of Populist and Populist Social parties, with a vote of 113,358, or 2.94 per cent, secured 4 seats.

11. The bewildering numbers, according to Couloumbis, *Political Reaction,* p. 134, were as follows: The Liberal Party headed by Venizelos; the Liberal Democratic Party headed by Papandreou; the Progressive Party of Markezinis; the Populist Social Party headed by Stephanos Stephanopoulos; the National Progressive Union of the Center headed by Papapolites; the Progressive Worker Farmer movement headed by Katsotas; the new Political Movement under Georgios Athanasiades-Novas (later appointed prime minister in 1965 but failing to secure confirmation); the Democratic Party headed by Allamanis; the Socialist Party headed by Tsirimokos; and the Agrarian Party led by Baltatzis.

12. In the 1961 elections, of the 4,333,411 valid ballots cast for the 300 seats, the National Radicals won 2,186,607 or 49.6 per cent and 174 seats (as compared to the Rally victory in 1952 with 49.22 per cent out of 1,591,807 valid ballots and 247 seats). The 174 deputies elected were later increased to 180 by the addition of four defectors from other parties. The Center Union and the Progressives together won 1,515,284 votes, or 34.3 per cent, and 103 seats. The Communist-dominated left under the name of Pan-Democratic Agrarian Front, secured 670,373 valid ballots, or 15.1 per cent of the total, and 23 seats. It went down from its 1958 record of 939,902 votes, or 24.42 per cent, of the total and 79 seats.

13. Couloumbis, *Political Reactions,* p. 143.

14. Heurtley, et al., *A Short History of Modern Greece from Early Times to 1964,* p. 178.

Chapter 8: From Right to Center and the New Left

1. A reliable source indicated that in November 1955 there were 4,498 Communists in prison after court conviction for murder or

other serious crimes committed during the Axis occupation, the uprising of December 3, 1944, and the 1945–1959 guerrilla war. During the same period an estimated 1,300 Communists had been deported to the islands.

2. In the 1963 elections, out of 4,579,146 valid ballots, a total of 1,931,289 or 42.18 per cent and 138 seats went to the Center Union; 1,786,008 or 39.01 per cent and 132 seats went to the National Radicals; 171,278 or 3.74 per cent and 2 seats to the Progressives, affiliated with the National Radicals; and 666,233 or 14.54 per cent and 28 seats to the United Democratic Left. A scattering of independents, with 24,338 votes, got no seats. Couloumbis, *Greek Political Reaction,* Appendix E, p. 232.

3. Mario S. Modiano, "Greek Political Troubles," *The World Today* (London: Royal Institute of International Affairs, Vol. 21, No. 1, January 1965), p. 37.

4. In 1964, out of a total of 4,504,818 valid ballots, the Center Union secured 2,377,647 or 52.78 per cent and 173 seats; the National Radicals, together with the Progressives, got 1,576,550 votes or 35 per cent of the total and 105 seats; the United Democratic Left, with 540,687 votes, dropped to 12 per cent and 22 seats. With 9,934 votes, the independent voters got no seats. The Center Union's 173 seats were later reduced to 171. Couloumbis, *Greek Political Reaction,* Appendix E, p. 232.

5. See *Statement of the Prime Minister, Mr. George Papandreou, on Plans for Educational Reform in Greece,* Prime Minister's Office, Press and Information Department, Athens, Nov. 16, 1963 (mimeographed); *Statement on Educational Reform Issued by the Prime Minister and Minister of Education,* Mr. George Papandreou, Prime Minister's Office, Press and Information Department, April 11, 1964 (mimeographed); and *Report on Education Developments in 1964–1965,* presented at the XXVIIIth session of the International Conference on Public Education, Geneva, July 1965, Ministry of National Education and Religion, published by the Division for International Cultural Relations, Athens, 1965. For text of legislation, see Legislative Decree 4379/1964 on the Organization and Administration of General Education, Ministry of National Education and Religion, Kingdom of Greece, Athens, 1964.

6. Kousoulas, *Revolution and Defeat,* p. 284. As of 1965, there were

reportedly 60,400 political refugees from Greece in the U.S.S.R. and other eastern European countries; of these, 30,000 were children, elderly or disabled; there were 5,690 young adults from the ages of 17 to 21 who had grown up in Communist countries to the north of Greece. Kousoulas, *Revolution and Defeat*, footnote 15, p. 284.

7. From 1952–1964, the Communist-dominated vote was as follows:

	No. of Votes	Percentage of Total
1952	152,011	9.55
1956	Left ran with other parties	
1958	939,902	24.42
1961	670,373	15.1
1963	666,233	14.54
1964	540,687	12.0

8. *New York Times*, August 7, 1966.

9. Ronald Layne, *Sunday Telegram* (London), April 23, 1967. See also Marcus Wheeler, "Greece: Grapes of Wrath," *The World Today* (London: Royal Institute of International Affairs), Vol. 23, No. 6, June 1967, *passim*.

Chapter 9: After Papandreou the Deluge

1. The Greek Constitution of 1952, translated by Alex. Tzinieris, Art. 70. (Mimeographed, undated.)

2. The king, as the supreme authority of the state, had the power to command "the armed forces, declare war, conclude treaties of peace and announce them to Parliament with the necessary clarifications when the interest and security of the nation permit." Constitution of 1952, Article 52.

3. *New York Times*, April 17, 1967.

4. October 26, 1966. See his earlier comments, especially August 5 and 8, 1965.

5. See letter from Professor J. H. Merryman, *New York Times*, October 17, 1966 and letters from a group of Cambridge University economists in *The Times* (London), May 3, 1967.

6. Constitution of 1952, Art. 31, which reads simply: "The King shall appoint and dismiss his Ministers."

7. Lord Campion et al., *Parliament: A Survey* (London: George Allen and Unwin), p. 39.

8. Constitution of 1952, Art. 78.

9. Art. 37. 10. Art. 38. 11. *Idem.* 12. Art. 29. See also Art. 36.

13. Art. 36. 14. Art. 37. 15. *Idem.* 16. *Le Monde* (Paris), September 18, 1965.

17. *The World Today*, June 1967, p. 237.

18. *The Economist*, Dec. 24, 1966. See also *idem.*, July 13, 1966.

19. Art. 62. 20. Art. 63. 21. *Ibid.*

22. The constitution gave the king power "in case of a state of war or mobilization due to external dangers or of a serious disturbance or of manifest threat to public order and to the security of the country from internal dangers" (Art. 91) to suspend certain articles of the constitution relating to civil liberties, but only on recommendation of the cabinet. By putting into effect a law on the state of siege, the king was also given power to establish extraordinary tribunals. All measures pertaining to such a crisis had to be announced to Parliament for approval or abrogation the first meeting after their promulgation (Art. 91). If any of the actions were taken when Parliament was not in session, the royal decree announcing them was required to summon Parliament to meet within ten days, even though its term were ended or it had been dissolved (Art. 91). In all cases except those involving war, the effect of the emergency decrees was required to end two months from their promulgation unless they had been extended meanwhile with Parliament's permission (Art. 91).

Selected Bibliography

Adamantis, Pepelasis, et al. *Economic Development: Analysis and Case Studies.* New York: Harper and Brothers, 1960.

Agency for International Development: *U.S. Overseas Loans and Grants and Assistance from International Organizations.* Washington, D.C.: July 1, 1945–June 30, 1966, March, 1967.

Albaugh, L. *Crete: A Case Study of an Underdeveloped Area.* Princeton, New Jersey: Princeton University Press, 1953.

Andreades, A. *Les effets économiques et sociales de la guerre en Grèce.* Paris, 1929.

Bank of Greece, *Annual Reports for the Years 1963–1966, Athens: General Statistics, Papers and Lectures.* Athens: 1963.
Monthly Statistical Bulletin. Athens: 1963.
Quarterly Reports. Athens: 1960–1966.

Barzanti, Sergio. *The Underdeveloped Areas within the Common Market.* Princeton, New Jersey: Princeton University Press, 1963.

Benns, F. Lee. *Europe Since 1914 in Its World Setting,* 6th and 8th Editions. New York: F. S. Crofts & Co., 1945.

Bowra, C. M. *The Greek Experience.* Cleveland: World Publishing Co., 1957.

Brown, William A., Jr., and Redvers, Opie. *American Foreign Assistance.* Washington, D.C.: Brookings Institution, 1953.

Bury, J. B. *A History of Greece.* New York: Modern Library, Random House, undated.

Center of Economic Research, Athens:
Alexander, Alec P. *Greek Industrialists: An Economic and Social Analysis.* (Research Monograph Series, 12). Athens: 1964.
Break, George F., and Ralph Turvey. *Studies in Greek Taxation* (Research Monograph Series, 11). Athens: 1964.

Coutsoumaris, George. *The Morphology of Greek Industry.* Athens: 1963.

Draft of the Five Year Economic Development Plan for Greece (1966–1970). Athens: December, 1965.

Draft of the Five Year Economic Development Plan for Greece, 1966–1970: A Summary. Athens: December, 1965.

Economic and Social Atlas on Greece, 1965.

Ellis, Howard S., in collaboration with Diomedes D. Psilos, Richard M. Westerbe, and Calliope Nicolaou. *Industrial Capital in Greek Development* (Research Monograph Series, 8). Athens: 1964.

Lambiri, Ioanna. *Social Change in a Greek Country Town* (Research Monograph Series, 13). Athens: 1965.

Papandreou, Andreas. *A Strategy for Greek Economic Development.* Athens: 1962.

Pepelasis, A. *Surplus Labor in Greek Agriculture, 1953–1960.* Athens: 1962.

Psilos, Diomedes D. *Capital Market in Greece* (Research Monograph Series, 9). Athens: 1964.

Suits, Daniel B. *An Econometric Model of the Greek Economy.* Athens: 1964.

Thompson, K. *Farm Fragmentation in Greece.* Athens: 1963.

Triantis, S. G. *Common Market and Economic Development:* E.E.C. and Greece (Research Monograph Series, 14). Athens: 1965.

Ward, Benjamin. *Greek Regional Development.* Athens: undated.

Coloumbis, Theodore A. *Greek Political Reaction to American and NATO Influences.* New Haven: Yale University Press, 1966.

Commercial Bank of Greece. *Annual Reports for the Years 1963–1966.*

Economic Bulletin. Athens: 1963–1966. (Quarterly.)

Cook, J. M. *The Greeks in Ionia and the East.* New York: Frederick A. Praeger, 1963.

Council of Europe Consultative Assembly. *Economic Developments of Southern Europe,* Report No. 1, Greece, Strasbourg, 1965.

Crawley, C. B. *The Question of Greek Independence: A Study of British Policy in the Near East, 1821–1839.* Cambridge: University Press, 1930.

FAO Mediterranean Development Project. Country Report, *Greece.* Rome, 1959.

Federation of Greek Industries (no author): Annual Reports on Greek Industry, 1963–1966.

Fermor, Patrick Leigh. *Mani: Travels in the Southern Peloponnese.* London: John Murray, 1958.

—————— *Roumeli: Travels in Northern Greece.* London: John Murray, 1966.

Finlay, G. *A History of Greece from Its Conquest by the Romans to the Present Time, B.C. 146 to A.D. 1864.* 7 vols. Oxford and London: Oxford University Press, 1877.

Finley, M. I., ed. *The Greek Historians.* New York: Viking Press, 1959.

Forster, Edward S. *A Short History of Modern Greece.* 3rd ed. London: Methuen & Co., Ltd., 1968.

Gardner, Ernest Arthur. *Greece and the Aegean.* London: George C. Harrep and Co., Ltd., 1933.

Greek Constitution of 1952, translated by Alex Tsinieris (mimeographed).

Griffith, William E., ed., *Communism in Europe.* Cambridge: The Massachusetts Institute of Technology Press, 1964.

Hadas, Moses, *Hellenistic Culture, Fusion and Diffusion.* New York: Columbia University Press, 1959.

Hamilton, Edith, *The Greek Way.* New York: W. W. Norton, 1930.

Haritou, Korisis, *Die politischen Parteien Griechenlands. Ein neuer Staat auf dem Weg zur Demokratie, 1821–1910.* Herzbrück/Nürnberg: Karl Pfeiffer, 1966.

Heurtley, W. A., H. C. Darby, C. W. Crawley, and C. M. Woodhouse. *A Short History of Greece from Early Times to 1966.* Cambridge: University Press, 1965.

Hoffman, Paul G. *World without Want.* New York: Harper & Row, 1962.

Institute for Balkan Studies, Thessaloniki, Greece:
Baxevanis, John. *The Port of Thessaloniki,* 1963.
Dakin, Douglas. *The Greek Struggle in Macedonia, 1897–1913,* 1966.
Dontas, Donna W. *The Last Phase of the War of Independence in Western Greece, 1827–1829,* 1966.

Jelavich, Barbara. *Russia and Greece during the Regency of King Othon,* 1966.

Kofos, Evangelos. *Nationalism and Communism in Macedonia,* 1964.

Negreponti-Delivanis, Maria W. *Le développement de la Grèce du Nord depuis 1913.* 1963.

Vouras, Paul P. *The Changing Economy of North Greece since World War II,* 1962.

Xydis, Stephen G. *Greece and the Great Powers, 1944–1947,* 1963.

International Labor Office, Geneva: "Labor Problems in Greece." *Report of the I.L.O. Mission.* Geneva, 1947.

Jelavich, Barbara. "Russia and the Greek Revolution of 1843," *Südosteuropeische Arbeiten,* 65. Munich: R. Oldenburg, 1966.

Kazantzakis, Nikos, *Freedom or Death.* New York: Simon and Schuster, 1961.

———— *Journey to the Morea.* New York, Simon and Schuster, 1965.

———— *Report to Greco.* New York, Simon and Schuster, 1965.

Kedros, André, *La Resistance Grecque, 1940–1944.* Paris: Robert Laffont, 1966.

Kousoulas, D. George. *The Price of Freedom: Greece in World Affairs, 1939–1953.* Syracuse: Syracuse University Press, 1953.

———— *Revolution and Defeat, The Story of the Greek Communist Party.* London: Oxford University Press, 1965.

Livingstone, Sir Richard Winn, ed. *The Legacy of Greece.* London: Oxford University Press, 1921.

Lowe, C. J. *Salisbury and the Mediterranean, 1886–1896.* London: Routledge & Kegan Paul, Ltd., 1965.

Mavrogordato, J. *Modern Greece, 1800–1931.* London: Macmillan and Co., Ltd., 1931.

McNeill, W. *Greece: American Aid in Action.* New York: Twentieth Century Fund, 1957.

Mead, Margaret, ed. *Cultural Patterns and Technical Change.* New York: Mentor Books, 1955 (prepared for UNESCO), Section II, Studies of Whole Cultures, *Greece,* pp. 57–96.

Miller, Helen Hill. *Bridge to Asia, The Greeks in the Eastern Mediterranean.* New York: Charles Scribner's Sons, 1967.

———— *Greece.* New York: Charles Scribner's Sons, 1961.

———— *Sicily and the Colonies of Western Greece.* New York: Charles Scribner's Sons, 1965.

Miller, William. *A History of the Greek People, 1821–31.* New York: E. P. Dutton and Co., 1923.

Ministry of Coordination, *Five-Year Programme for the Economic Development of Greece, 1960–1966:* Athens: April, 1961.

———— *Legislative Decree 4379/1964 on the Organization and Administration of General Education.* Athens: 1964.

———— *Report on Education During the School Year 1963–1964 Presented to the XXVIIth International Conference for Public Education, Geneva, July 1964.* Athens: 1964.

Ministry of National Education and Religion. *Greece: Education.* Athens (undated, mimeographed).

———— *The Organization and Administration of General Education,* Athens: National Printing Office, 1965.

Munkman, C. A. *American Aid to Greece. A Report on the First Ten Years.* New York: Frederick A. Praeger, 1958.

Myers, Edmund Charles Wolf. *Greek Entanglement.* London: Hart-Davis, 1955.

Nagel. *Nagel's Travel Guide to Greece.* Geneva: Taplinger Publishing Co., Inc., 1962.

National Bank of Greece:
Annual Reports for the years 1963–1966, Athens.
"Greece Today." *Monthly Economic and Statistical Review, 1963–1966.* Athens.
Quarterly Review. 1960–1964, especially Year IV, No. 13–14, "A Decade of Economic Progress," Athens.

National Statistical Service of Greece. *Statistical Yearbook of Greece.* Athens: 1963, 1964, 1965, 1966.

Near East Foundation, New York: Badeau, John S. and Georgianna G. Stevens, ed. *Bread from Stones, Fifty Years of Technical Assistance.* (Especially, Chapter V, Basil G. Moussouros, "Education in Greece.") Englewood Cliffs, New Jersey: Prentice-Hall, Inc., 1966.

O'Ballance, Edgar. *The Greek Civil War, 1944–1949.* London: Faber and Faber, Ltd., 1964.

Organization for European Economic Cooperation and Development. *Agricultural Policies in Europe and North America, First Report,* Paris: Ministerial Committee for Food and Agriculture, May, 1956.

"Greece." *Economic Surveys by the OECD.* Paris, 1963–1967.

"Greece." *OECD Country Reports, Education and Development.* The Mediterranean Regional Project. Paris: 1965.

Reorganization of Public Administration in Greece, a Report by Professor Georges Langrod, Problems of Development Series. Paris: undated, 1964 or 1965.

Ostrogorsky, George. *History of the Byzantine State.* New Brunswick, N.J.: Rutgers University Press, 1957.

Papagos, Field Marshal Alexander. *The Battle of Greece, 1940–1941.* Athens: I. M. Scazikis, "Alpha" Editions, 1949 (in English).

Pfeffer, Karl Heinz and Iram Schaffhausen. *Griechenland.* Hamburg: Grenzen Wirtschaftlicher Hilfe für Entwicklungserfolg, 1959.

Prime Minister's Office, Foreign Press Division:
   King of Greece as the Head of the State. Athens: September 1953 (mimeographed).
   Negas, George A. *Greek Calendar Customs.* Athens: 1958 (mimeographed).
   Releases 1960–1964. Athens: February 1963 (mimeographed).
   Statements of Prime Minister. Athens: 1962–1966 (mimeographed).

Public Power Corporation:
   Report of the Board of Directors for the Fiscal Year 1954–1955, with a General Review of the Five-Year Period 1951–1955. Athens: undated.
   The First Ten Years. Athens: undated.

Rand, Christopher. *Grecian Calendar.* New York: Oxford University Press, Inc., 1962.

Renner, E. J. "Erosion, Trojan Horse of Greece," *National Geographic,* December 1, 1957.

Report of the FAO Mission for Greece. Food and Agricultural Organization of the United Nations, Washington, D.C., March, 1947.

Rossi-Doria, Manlio. "Agriculture and Europe," *The New Europe,* in *Daedalus,* Winter 1964.

Runciman, Steven. *The Fall of Constantinople, 1453.* Cambridge: University Press, 1965

Sanders, Irwin T. *Rainbow in the Rock: The People of Rural Greece.* Cambridge: Harvard University Press, 1962.

Smathers, Frank, William McNeill, and Elizabeth McNeill. *Report on the Greeks.* New York: Twentieth Century Fund, 1958.

Spencer, Floyd A. *War and Post-War Greece: An Analysis Based on Greek Writings.* Washington, D.C.: Library of Congress, 1952.

Stewart, I. McD. G. *The Struggle for Crete, 20 May–1 June 1941.* London: Oxford University Press, 1966.

Sweet-Escott, Bickham. *Greece, a Political and Economic Survey, 1939–1953.* London and New York: Royal Institute of International Affairs, 1954.

United Nations Economic Commission for Europe. *Economic Survey of Europe in 1948.* Geneva: May, 1949.

——— *Economic Survey of Europe in 1953,* including a study of economic development in Southern Europe. Geneva: February, 1954.

——— *Economic Survey of Europe in 1963,* Geneva: March, 1964.

United States Embassy. Unclassified Documents. Athens: February and October, 1963.

United States Information Service. Konold, Kristine. *Brief Survey of Elementary and Education Institutions in Greece.* Athens: November, 1952.

Venizelos, Eleutherios and Others. *The Vindication of Greek National Policy, 1912–1917.* London: George Allen and Unwin Ltd., 1918.

Voight, F. A. *The Greek Sedition.* London: Hollis & Carter, 1949.

Ward, Barbara. *The Rich Nations and the Poor Nations.* New York: W. W. Norton, 1962.

Woodhouse, C. M. *Apple of Discord. A Survey of Recent Greek Politics in their International Setting.* London: Hutchinson & Co., Ltd., 1948.

——— *The Greek War of Independence.* London: Longmans, Green and Co., Ltd., 1952.

Xydis, Stephen G., *Cyprus: Conflict and Conciliation, 1954–1958.* Columbus: Ohio State University Press, 1967.

Zimmern, Alfred. *The Greek Commonwealth. Politics and Economics in 5th Century Athens.* Oxford: Clarendon Press, 1931.

Zotos, Stephanos, *Greece: The Struggle for Freedom, the Courageous Story of Greek Resistance to Fascism, Nazism, and Communism, 1940–1949.* New York: Thomas Y. Crowell Co., 1967.

Index